WILD GAME

MADE EASY

Chef John Schumacher
The Game Gourmet®

International
Cuisine Publishers

Foreword

*Chef John with
daughter Brandi*

As a chef and hunter, I have been cooking wild game dishes for 30 years. The dreaming, planning, traveling and time spent in nature all contribute to the excitement and fulfillment of hunting.

This book was written to help you continue the joy of the hunt and complete the experience.

Many cooks are intimidated by the thought of preparing wild game. The principles are simple. Game meats are often stored improperly and for too long a period of time. They need to be roasted at low heat or grilled and sautéed at moderate heat and should be served with complementary flavors.

These recipes have been carefully crafted to create culinary successes. They will provide you with an opportunity to expose hunters and non-hunters to the unique flavors of fowl and game.

I wish you the best in completing the joy of the hunt!

Chef John
The Game Gourmet®

Also available, a companion video. Send $15.95 plus $3.50 shipping and insurance to:
International Culinary Publishers,
212 W. Main Street,
New Prague, MN 56071

CREDITS

Mike Vail
Vice President,
Products & Business Development

Dan Kennedy
Book Production Manager

Gina Seeling
Book Design

Joe Fahey
Book Design Assistant

Kim Baily
Photography

ISBN 0-914697-87-0

2 3 4 5 6 / 02 01 00 99

North American Hunting Club
12301 Whitewater Drive
Minnetonka, Minnesota 55343

Contents

WILD GAME MADE EASY

Breakfast for
Home & Camp

Fast Larry's Griddle Cakes Stack-Ups
Side dish: Venison Sausage

FAST LARRY'S GRIDDLE CAKES STACK-UPS

1 lb. ground venison meat
2 T. olive oil
1 16-oz. jar spaghetti sauce
4 cups of your favorite pancake batter
2 cups shredded mozzarella or Swiss cheese

Serves 4 hunters

Heat a skillet until very hot. Add venison and oil. Cook until brown. Drain off excess oil. Add spaghetti sauce and bring to a boil.

Make 3 medium-size pancakes in another skillet. Place one on a plate. Top with about ⅓ cup sauce. Add second pancake. Top with more sauce. Add third pancake. Top with sauce and ½ cup cheese. Serve.

BLOW-UP PANCAKES

BATTER:
½ cup milk
2 eggs, slightly beaten
½ cup all-purpose flour
¼ tsp. salt
1 T. butter

FILLING:
2 T. butter
1 cup sliced mushrooms
1 cup diced game sausage or salami
½ cup diced red pepper
½ tsp. Worcestershire sauce
¼ tsp. seasoned salt
¼ tsp. black pepper
1 cup Swiss or Muenster cheese, shredded

Heat oven to 425°

HINT

Of course, this is great with tomato salsa or spaghetti sauce. Fresh horse-radish is also an eye opener!

To make batter: In a bowl, whisk the milk and eggs to combine. Add flour and salt. Whisk to make a smooth batter (no lumps, please).

In a deep 9″ or 10″ pie pan, melt butter. When butter is melted, add batter to pan and bake for 12-15 minutes, until golden brown.

To make filling: While pancake is baking, melt 2 tablespoons butter in a heavy skillet. Add mushrooms, sausage and red pepper. Cook until pepper is tender. Add Worcestershire sauce, salt and black pepper. When pancake is getting brown, place half the cheese over it.

Add filling and top with remaining cheese. Return to oven. Bake for 5 minutes. Remove and let set 5 minutes before serving.

Hunter's Quiche
Side dish: Salsa

HUNTERS DO EAT QUICHE

1 pie crust (see recipe p. 188)
¼ cup chopped fresh green onions
1½ cups cheddar cheese shredded
1½ cups cooked leftover duck, goose or pheasant, cut into ¼″ cubes
1 cup fresh asparagus, cut into ½″ pieces
1 cup venison sausage links or summer sausage, sliced ⅛″ thick
4 eggs
2 egg yolks
1½ cups half-and-half
1 tsp. salt
¼ tsp. black pepper

Makes one pie

Make pie crust dough, adding chopped fresh green onions to dough. Roll out dough to ⅛″ thickness and place in a 10″ pie plate. Place cheese, fowl pieces, asparagus pieces and sausage in the bottom. In a bowl, whisk the eggs, yolks, half-and-half, salt and pepper to a smooth liquid and pour over filling.

Place in a 375° oven for about 45 minutes, or until set. Let stand 10 minutes. This will be a very full pie. Bake on a sheet or cookie pan. Serve with salsa.

HINTS

If you are not using fowl, use any cooked ground game.

EGGS BENEDICT ELK TENDERLOINS

8 pieces elk tenderloin, 1″ thick
4 cups hollandaise sauce
(see recipe p. 175)
1 T. olive oil

1 T. Worcestershire sauce
8 eggs
4 English muffins, halved and toasted
4 black olives, cut in half

Flatten elk pieces lightly with a meat mallet. Make the hollandaise sauce.

Heat oil in a large skillet. Add tenderloins and brown. Turn meat over and cook to medium rare. Splash with Worcestershire sauce. While preparing the steaks, poach the eggs to soft stage.

To assemble: Place two English muffin halves on a plate. Top each half with an elk steak, one poached egg, ½ cup hollandaise sauce and ½ black olive. Serve immediately.

This recipe works well with any tenderloin or even split, flattened pheasant breast. The reason we add the Worcestershire sauce to the frying meat is to stop the browning process.

Moose Leg Red Hash
Side dish: Baking Powder Biscuits

MOOSE LEG RED HASH

2 cups red potatoes, with skins on
1½ cups cubed moose roast, in
¼" cubes
1 T. olive oil
1 cup red onion, diced
1 clove garlic, minced

1 tsp. salt
½ tsp. black pepper
1 cup chili sauce
½ cup barbecue sauce
½ cup diced dill pickles

HINTS

Any red game meat will taste great.

Boil and cool potatoes. Cut into ¼" cubes. Remember to remove fat and silver skin from moose meat. Heat oil in a skillet until almost smoke hot. Add meat and brown it. Add onion, garlic, salt, pepper. Cook until onion is tender.

Add chili sauce, barbecue sauce and dill pickles. Bring to a boil. Let simmer 2 minutes. Add potatoes. Reduce heat to low and cook until potatoes are hot. Stir very gently and serve.

I like mine with poached eggs and rye toast.

VENISON PATTIES

1 lb. ground venison meat
¼ cup fresh bread crumbs
(see recipe p. 172)
1 tsp. dry thyme leaves
1 tsp. onion salt

1 tsp. freshly ground black pepper
1 lb. bulk pork sausage
1 egg, beaten
oil

Use up ground game by freezing uncooked patties. Place on wax paper or plastic wrap. Use any flavor sausage you wish. Add your favorite spices or peppers.

If you are grinding your own venison, remove fat, excess silver skin and sinews. Chill venison until almost frozen. This makes the soft venison grind better.

In a large bowl, combine bread crumbs, thyme, onion salt and pepper. Add ground venison, pork sausage and egg. Mix well to combine, making sure there are no dry bread crumbs. Rub a little oil on your hands and make patties. Make 6 to 8 patties. Press each patty to ⅓" thickness. Pan-fry patties slowly until they are thoroughly cooked. Drain fat as patties cook.

Applesauce serves as a nice accompaniment. I top these on the grill with Swiss cheese or pineapple rings and serve with bacon, lettuce and tomato on a hard roll.

GAMEKEEPER BLANKETS

8 large crêpes, the size of a plate (see following recipe)

POTATO FILLING:
2 cups halved, peeled potatoes
½ cup sour cream
1 tsp. ground nutmeg

GAME FILLING:
1 T. oil
1 lb. ground venison meat

2 cloves minced garlic
1 cup chopped onion
1 10½-oz. can mushroom soup
1 tsp. thyme
1 tsp. salt
½ tsp. black pepper
½ cup frozen green peas

Serves 4 (2 crêpes each)

Boil, drain and cool the potatoes slightly. Add sour cream and nutmeg, then mash potatoes. Place in a covered bowl.

Heat oil in a large heavy skillet until hot. Add ground venison and garlic. Cook until meat is brown. Add onion and cook until onion is clear and soft. Drain off all liquid. Add soup, thyme, salt and pepper. Stir with wooden spoon and simmer for 5 minutes. Add peas. Combine well.

To assemble: Lay crêpes out flat. Spread ⅓ cup mashed potato mixture evenly on top. In the center place 1 cup meat mixture and gently fold four sides of crepes gently in. Serve and smile.

You didn't hear this from me, but they taste great with ketchup.

CRÊPES

1½ cups half-and-half
1 T. oil or melted butter
2 eggs

1 cup all-purpose flour
¼ tsp. salt

Place liquids in bowl and combine well. Add dry ingredients and beat until smooth. It is best to use a wire whisk or hand beater.

Heat a nonstick pan. Remove from heat and add ¼ cup batter.

Lift and tilt the pan to spread batter. Return to heat and cook to a light brown. Turn crêpe and cook to a light brown. If crêpe darkens too quickly, reduce heat.

Crêpes may be filled with jam, jelly, fruit or cheese of choice. They can be rolled and served with syrup, whipped cream, ice cream or meat filling. After I turn crêpes, I place a thin slice of farmer's cheese in the center, roll up the crêpe and enjoy.

HINT

I use an electric fry pan at 350°. You may stack crêpes after cooling and freeze for later use.

PHEASANT NEST OMELETS

6 eggs
¼ cup milk
1 tsp. salt
1 pinch white pepper
1 tsp. Worcestershire sauce
1 T. butter

2 cups diced cooked pheasant meat,
¼" cubes
2 cups diced cooked broccoli,
½" cubes
1 cup diced fresh tomatoes,
½" pieces salsa

Serves 4

In a bowl, beat together eggs, milk, salt and white pepper. Heat a large nonstick pan until hot. Add butter and cook butter to a golden brown. Add pheasant and broccoli pieces.

Sauté until hot. Add egg mixture and cook just until egg starts to thicken. Scramble eggs. Place tomato pieces in center. Remove from heat.

Cover 1 minute. Place on a large platter and serve.

HINT

Fresh salsa goes extremely well with these. You may use your favorite cheese as an additional topping, or add sour cream and green onions.

ONE-EYED JACKS

BATTER:
3 eggs
½ cup half-and-half
2 T. brown sugar
1 tsp. vanilla
1 tsp. ground cinnamon

To make batter: Place all ingredients in a large bowl and whisk until smooth.

8 slices cinnamon bread cut ½" thick
1 T. butter
8 eggs

Serve 2 slices per person with syrup, jam and fried apples.

Cut center from bread slices with a 3" round cookie cutter. Heat skillet over medium heat. Add ½ tablespoon butter. Dip 4 slices bread, one at a time, in batter shaking off excess batter. Place slices in skillet. Break one egg in the center of each piece and fry until egg coagulates and bread is golden brown. Turn and fry to desired doneness.

LOOK
INSIDE!

Game Sauerkraut Balls

Game Zucchini Canoes

Schumacher's
Hotel Pâté

Mini Game Tostados

SCHUMACHER'S HOTEL PÂTÉ

1 lb. livers
(duck, goose or upland game bird)
4 cups water
1½ cups diced onion
2 bay leaves

1½ tsp. ground allspice, divided
⅔ cup mayonnaise (or Miracle Whip)
⅓ cup cream cheese
salt to taste

Serves 4

The first thing to do in making this recipe is to rinse the livers very well. If you don't rinse the livers, the pâté will have a bitter taste. (It is also a good rule to thoroughly rinse any liver used for cooking.)

Split livers and trim off all fat and connective tissue. Wash and rinse and place in a heavy medium pot with water, onion, bay leaves and 1 teaspoon allspice. Cover and simmer on low heat until livers are cooked and tender. Run cold water over livers and onion until cool and well-rinsed. Remove bay leaves. Chop liver and onion fine in a food processor. Add mayonnaise, cream cheese, ½ teaspoon allspice and salt to taste. Mix until smooth. Cool and serve with sliced hard-boiled eggs and capers.

Prepare this dish 3 to 5 hours before serving. Its flavor becomes fuller as it chills.

GAME ZUCCHINI CANOES

1 lb. ground game meat
1 cup minced onion
2 cloves garlic, minced
2 cups shredded sharp cheddar cheese

1 tsp. black pepper, freshly ground
4 zucchini, each about 6-8″ long
1 cup shredded pepper cheese

Serves 4-6

In a skillet, cook game with onion and garlic until onion is tender and meat is browned. Drain the liquid. Add cheddar cheese and black pepper. Stir to combine.

Cut zucchini in half lengthwise. Remove seeds with a spoon making a trench in the middle, starting ½″ from the ends.

Fill trench with a generous amount of meat mixture. Sprinkle with shredded pepper cheese and bake at 375° for 15 minutes.

HINTS

I found that the slightly sweeter flavor of Miracle Whip works well and is also less likely to spoil.

Serve whole zucchini cut into 4 pieces for small appetites.

GAME SAUERKRAUT BALLS

2 T. butter
½ cup diced onion
¼ cup finely shredded carrot
2 cups ground game meat
4 cups chopped sauerkraut, well drained
1 cup ground ham
1⅔ cups all-purpose divided flour
¼ cup heavy cream
¼ cup beef stock (see recipe p. 186)

1 tsp. caraway seeds (optional)
½ tsp. allspice
¼ tsp. salt
¼ tsp. white pepper
¼ tsp. dry mustard
4 eggs, beaten
2 cups fresh bread crumbs
(see recipe p. 172)
oil for deep fat frying

Serves 4-6

HINTS

Frozen sauerkraut, thawed and well drained, has the best flavor.

In a frying pan, melt butter. Add onions and carrots and sauté until tender. Add game and brown. Add sauerkraut and ham. Cook 5 minutes on low heat. Sprinkle in ⅔ cup flour while stirring and cook until thick. If your sauerkraut mixture is too loose to form balls, add more flour. Add heavy cream, stock and spices.

Cook on low heat for 5 minutes, stirring occasionally to keep from burning. Remove from pan and place on a cookie sheet to cool. When completely cool and firm, make into balls the size of walnuts (about 1″ diameter). Roll in 1 cup flour, then dip into beaten eggs. Roll in bread crumbs. Deep-fry balls in 375° oil until golden brown.

MINI GAME TOSTADOS

1 T. olive oil
2 cloves garlic, minced
½ cup red onion, cut matchstick size
½ cup carrots, cut matchstick size
2 cups diced cooked game meat
1 tsp. chili powder

1 bag of large tortilla chips
½ cup refried beans
½ cup hot salsa
½ cup guacamole
1 cup cheddar cheese, shredded

I keep diced leftover game or fowl in a small freezer bag just for this use. And, of course, use this recipe for tacos.

In a skillet, heat oil and garlic. When garlic starts to brown, add onion, and carrots. Cook 1 minute. Add meat cubes and chili powder; toss gently. Remove from heat.

Lay unbroken chips on a baking sheet. Top each chip with 1 teaspoon refried beans, 1 tablespoon meat mixture, 1 teaspoon salsa, 1 teaspoon guacamole and 2 teaspoons cheddar cheese. Bake at 375° until cheese is melted and beans are hot.

Use diced dill pickles and hot peppers as toppings too.

CAJUN GAME WINGS WITH PINEAPPLE SAUCE

16 wings from game birds
2 cups crushed pineapple, with liquid
¼ cup cider vinegar
¼ cup horseradish
2 T. soy sauce
2 T. olive oil

½ tsp. cayenne pepper
2 cloves garlic, minced
⅓ cup honey
1 T. cornstarch
¼ cup dry red wine

Use wings from any game bird. Remove all pin feathers and cut at center joint. Remove tip. From each wing, you will have 2 pieces. Discard tip ends or save them for stock.

In a glass bowl, place wings, pineapple, vinegar, horseradish, soy sauce, olive oil, cayenne pepper and garlic. Cover and marinate 2 days. Remove wings from marinade (save marinade). Place on a cookie sheet, and bake at 375° until wings are tender. Remove wings to covered dish. Combine marinade and honey in a saucepan. Dissolve cornstarch in red wine and add to sauce. Bring to a slow boil to thicken. When thick and clear, add sauce to wings and serve.

HINT

Use the same size wings. Goose wings work well. They just take longer to bake.

EASY STICKING GAME CUBES

1 lb. red game meat, cut into 1″ cubes
1 T. olive oil
1 14-oz. bottle chili sauce
2 T. dill pickle juice
1 tsp. honey

1 tsp. lemon juice
1 tsp. molasses
1 tsp. dry thyme
1 tsp. lemon pepper
¼ tsp. hot sauce

Remove fat and silver skin from game. Cut game into 1″ cubes. Heat olive oil until smoke hot. Add cubes and brown on all sides. Pour off excess oil. Add remaining ingredients. Combine well. Bring to a boil and simmer for 5 minutes.

Transfer to a warm serving bowl. Toothpicks work great for stabbing and serving.

The meat will be chewy but it has great flavor.
The most tender cuts work best.

HINT

Of course, it works very well as an entrée or in a submarine roll as a sandwich.

JUST FOR FUN GAME PORCUPINE MEATBALLS

1 lb. ground game meat
½ lb. ground pork
⅔ cup uncooked long-grain rice
½ cup diced onion
½ cup dry red wine
1½ tsp. garlic salt
1 tsp. black pepper, freshly ground

1 tsp. chili powder
2 cups plain spaghetti sauce
1 T. vegetable oil
1 cup beef stock (see recipe p. 186)
2 tsp. Worcestershire sauce
3 drops hot sauce

In a large bowl, combine game, pork, rice, onion, red wine, salt, pepper and chili powder.

Shape into 1½″ meatballs, making sure they are pressed firm. Heat oil in a skillet and brown meatballs. Gently place meatballs in a casserole dish.

Combine spaghetti sauce, beef stock, Worcestershire sauce and hot sauce, and pour over meatballs. Cover dish and bake at 350° for 1 hour. Test for doneness. When rice is tender and meat is no longer pink, remove and serve with Italian bread sticks or fresh bread to dip in the sauce.

This is an excellent appetizer.

VENISON AND HERBED GOAT CHEESE LOGS

3-lb. boneless venison roast
1 cup soft goat cheese
1 T. olive oil
1 tsp. Worcestershire sauce
1 tsp. chopped fresh tarragon

1 tsp. chopped fresh basil
½ tsp. freshly ground black pepper
½ tsp. dry thyme
½ tsp. dry sage
2 drops hot sauce

Trim off all fat and silver skin from roast. Place meat on rack in a roaster pan. Bake roast at 250° to internal temperature of 130° for medium rare. Remove and chill overnight.

With a sharp knife, slice roast across the grain as thin as you can.

In bowl, combine remaining ingredients to make a thick paste. Lay end piece of meat out flat and place 1 tablespoon. filling on one end. Roll up into tiny logs. These can be made 1 day ahead but must be kept tightly covered!

This takes some time and preparation, but it is well worth it.
It is very important to use a roast from a hind leg with no
sinews running through it.

GRILLED PHEASANT FINGERS WITH CASHEW APPLESAUCE

2 boneless, skinless pheasant breasts

MARINADE:
1 cup orange juice
1 cup coconut flakes
1 T. minced peeled fresh ginger
1 T. fresh lemon juice
2 tsp. curry powder
3 drops hot sauce

SAUCE:
½ cup applesauce
½ cup cashew pieces
½ cup smooth peanut butter
2 T. fresh lime juice
2 T. soy sauce
1 tsp. brown sugar
1 clove garlic
3 drops hot sauce (or to taste)
½ tsp. salt
25 bamboo skewers (7″ long)

Serves 4

Cut pheasant breasts into strips the size of your little finger.

Place all marinade ingredients in a blender and blend for 1 minute. Place marinade in a sealable bag with pheasant fingers. Refrigerate overnight.

Place all sauce ingredients in a blender and blend until smooth.

To prepare, soak skewers in water for 30 minutes. Thread pheasant fingers on accordian-style skewers. Grill over medium heat until done, about 2 minutes on each side. Serve with dipping sauce.

You can also cook this under the broiler.
Place a sheet of foil over each skewer end to keep from burning the wood.

HINT

This recipe also works very well with red game strips. Use only the most tender cuts.

UPLAND GAME STOCK

3½ lbs. upland game birds
4 qts. water
2 cups chopped onions
1½ cups chopped celery
1 sachet bag (see p. 186)

Wash game birds and cut into quarters. Place all ingredients in a large soup pot. Simmer on low heat for 3½ hours, skimming off fat and foam from time to time. Remove from heat and strain.

Put only the liquid back in the pot and return to a rolling boil until liquid has been reduced by half. Skim off fat. Cool and store.

Do not simmer longer than 4 hours or stock will taste bitter.

GAME STRUDEL

1 lb. ground game meat
2 cups diced onions
2 cups diced carrots
2 cups diced potatoes
2 cloves garlic, minced fine
2 T. all-purpose flour
1½ tsp. dry basil

1½ tsp. onion salt
½ tsp. black pepper
3 drops hot sauce
1 10½-oz. can cream of tomato soup
12 sheets phyllo dough
½ cup olive oil

Serves 4-6

In a heavy soup pot, brown meat. Add onions, carrots, potatoes and garlic. Cover and steam on low heat until potatoes just start to get tender. (Potatoes are better under-cooked than over-cooked.) Add flour, basil, salt and pepper and hot sauce. Gently combine to make stiff mixture. Add tomato soup and gently combine. Remove to bowl and let cool in refrigerator for 1 hour.

Layer 6 sheets of phyllo for each strudel, drizzling olive oil between sheets. Do the same with remaining 6 sheet. Place half of game mixture in center of each set of layered sheets. Enclose by first folding over, lengthwise, then fold the 2 short sides in and roll over so seam is down.

Brush each strudel with remaining oil and bake on cookie sheet at 350° for 40 minutes. Cool slightly before serving.

I like to serve this with fresh horseradish or horseradish sauce.

Mushroom-Stuffed Game Mountains

8 large mushrooms
4 bacon slices, diced
1 cup ground game meat
½ cup diced shallots
½ tsp. black pepper, freshly ground
½ tsp. dry rosemary, crushed
¼ cup fresh bread crumbs (see recipe p. 172)
⅓ cup chopped stuffed olives
1 tsp. onion salt
½ cup cream cheese, at room temperature
olive oil spray
½ cup dry white wine
2 cloves garlic, minced

HINT

I sometimes sprinkle grated cheese on top of this delicious appetizer.

Wash mushrooms. Remove stems and dice them (the finer the better). Set caps aside.

In a heavy skillet, brown bacon. Remove pieces to a paper-towel-lined plate with a slotted spoon. Add game and shallots to skillet and brown. Add diced mushroom stems, garlic, pepper and rosemary. Cook on low heat for 5 minutes. Add bread crumbs and cooked bacon; combine well. Stir with wooden spoon to keep from burning. Remove to a bowl to cool.

In a bowl, combine cream cheese, olives and onion salt. When mixture is soft, add to meat mixture and combine well. Spray outside of mushroom caps with olive oil spray. Stuff each mushroom with a generous mound of filling so they look like mountains.

Place stuffed caps side by side in a cake pan. Add ½ cup white wine to pan and bake at 350° for 30 minutes. Transfer to a plate and serve.

If your mushroom caps are very large, add an additional ½ cup wine to pan.

COWBOY MEAT CLEAVERS

8 bone-in game loin chops
1 cup smokey barbecue sauce
2 oz. (¼ cup) tequila

1 jalapeño pepper, stem removed
1 tsp. dry sage
1 tsp. freshly ground black pepper

Trim all fat and silver skin off meat. Trim all meat and fat off one end of bone. The chop will look like a meat cleaver. Some people call this Frenching.

Place remaining ingredients in a blender. Blend 1 minute. Place chops and sauce in sealable bag and refrigerate for 1 day.

Remove chops from sauce and wipe all sauce from bones. Wrap bones in foil to keep from burning. Grill over medium heat to medium rare.

Remove foil and serve chops on a hot platter. The bone is used to hold the chop.

Use as many jalapeño peppers as you can take for heat.
Good luck, cowboy!

TURTLE SOUP

5 cups water
1½ lbs. turtle meat, cubed ¼"
1½ tsp. salt
¼ tsp. hot sauce
1 cup white onion, diced
2 cloves garlic, minced
⅓ cup butter
1 cup diced red onions

⅓ cup all-purpose flour
1 cup medium-hot tomato salsa
¼ cup tomato purée
¼ cup lemon juice
2 T. Worcestershire sauce
2 hard-cooked eggs, coarsely chopped
1 T. capers, drained
1 T. dry parsley flakes

In a soup pot, place turtle meat, water, salt and hot sauce. Bring to a boil. Cook on a low rolling boil for 10 minutes.

Reduce heat and skim off foam and fat. Add white onion and garlic. Simmer about 2 hours, covered. Skim one more time.

In a skillet, heat butter to a fast bubble. Add red onion and cook until tender. Add flour and cook 2 minutes on low, stirring to keep from burning. Add salsa. Combine and add all to soup base. Add tomato purée, lemon juice and Worcestershire sauce and simmer for 20 minutes.

Serve in a bowl topped with chopped eggs, capers and parsley flakes.

WILD DUCK BORSCHT

2 small or 1 large duck, or 1 small goose (skin removed)
5 cups cold water
3 cups green cabbage (1 small head)
3 cups tomato juice
1 cup diced onion
1 cup diced carrots
1 cup diced beets (drained but save the juice)
1 cup beet juice
1 cup cooked or canned butter beans, drained
1 T. cider vinegar
1 T. beef base
2 cloves garlic, minced
2 tsp. chopped fresh dill weed
1 tsp. salt
½ tsp. black pepper
2 cups diced potatoes (skins on)
sour cream for garnish

Serves 6-8

Clean and cut ducks into 6 pieces. (If using a large duck or small goose, cut into 8 pieces by splitting breast in half.)

Place all ingredients except potatoes, in a slow cooker. Cover and cook for 3 hours. Add potatoes. Cook 1 hour. When meat falls from the bone, soup is done. Adjust flavor with salt and pepper. Serve in bowls with a large dollop of sour cream.

HINT

If you wish, substitute 2 cups liquid with 1 bottle German beer.

WILD CHILI TURKEY SOUP

4 cups diced turkey
¼ cup olive oil
1 cup chopped red peppers
1 clove garlic, minced
½ cup chopped onion
2 T. all-purpose flour
½ tsp. ground cumin
3 cups beef stock (see recipe p. 186)
3 cups diced tomato and juice
¼ cup dry red wine
2 cups canned chili beans
1 cup butter beans, drained
½ cup chopped green onions
2 T. chili powder
1 tsp. salt
1 tsp. black pepper
1 avocado, cut into in ½" cubes
1 cup shredded pepper cheese
1 cup sour cream

Serves 8

Remove all skin, sinews and bones from turkey. Heat half the oil in a large heavy soup pot. Add turkey and brown. Remove turkey and set aside.

Add remaining oil to skillet. Heat over medium heat. Add red pepper , onion and garlic, and sauté, until tender. Combine flour and cumin. Add to vegetables. Cook for 1 minute stirring gently to keep from sticking.

Add turkey pieces, beef stock, and chopped tomatoes and wine. Simmer on low heat for 45 minutes. Add beans and green onions. Combine gently and simmer for 15 minutes. Add chili powder, salt and pepper.

Serve with cubed avocado, shredded pepper cheese and sour cream as garnishes.

I use the thigh, wings and leg meat from the turkey.
I use all my upland game bird parts for this.

WILD RICE DUCK SOUP

4 cups cubed duck meat, ½″ cubes   6 cups chicken stock
¼ cup butter   (see recipe p. 186)
1 cup diced onion   2 10½-oz. cans cream of celery soup
1 cup diced celery   1½ cups uncooked wild rice
1 cup diced carrots   1 cup dry white wine
2 bay leaves   ½ tsp. freshly ground black pepper

HINT

Make this soup a day in advance. Cover and refrigerate. You can reheat it and serve. It also freezes well.

Debone and remove the skin, fat, silver skin and sinews from duck. Cut duck into cubes. In soup pot, heat butter to a fast bubble. Add duck and brown well. Add onion, celery and carrots. Cook until vegetables are tender. Add remaining ingredients and simmer uncovered on low heat for 1½ hours, or until wild rice is tender.

GOOSE POTATO CORN CHOWDER

BASE: 1 T. all-purpose flour
1 large goose, cut into 6 pieces   3 cups cream-style corn
8 cups water   2 cups cubed potatoes, ½″ cubes
1 cup coarsely chopped onion, cut   1 cup frozen corn kernels
in 2″ chunks   2 T. Worcestershire sauce
1 sachet bag (see recipe p. 186)   1 T. chicken base
½ lb. bacon, diced   1½ tsp. dry thyme
1 cup diced onion   ½ tsp. black pepper

Serves 4-6

Skin goose and cut into 6 pieces. In a soup pot, place goose, water, onion chunks and sachet bag. Simmer for 2 hours. Remove goose pieces from broth and debone. Cut meat into 1″ cubes. Strain broth. Skim all fat off the top. Place liquid in clean soup pot and simmer to reduce broth to 5 cups.

In a skillet, brown bacon. Add diced onions and cook until tender. Add flour and combine well. Cook on low heat for 2 minutes. Add to the goose broth and stir well. Add remaining ingredients and cubed meat. Simmer on low heat for 30 minutes. Adjust the seasoning by adding salt.

You may use duck or 2 small geese.
It is very important to skim off all fat from broth.

Game Gumbo Soup

GAME GUMBO SOUP

2¹/₂ cups cubed game or fowl
¹/₃ cup olive oil
¹/₃ cup all-purpose flour
2 cups chopped onions
2 cloves garlic, minced
3 cups whole tomatoes with juice
4 hot Italian sausages, sliced
2 cups okra, sliced
1 cup tomato juice
1 cup tomato sauce
2 tsp. beef base
1 tsp. filé powder
1 tsp. paprika
1 tsp. dry thyme
1 tsp. dry oregano
1 tsp. freshly ground black pepper

Serves 4

HINT

With a wooden spoon, gently stir soup from time to time while cooking. This soup reheats well.

Clean and remove skin, bones, fat, silver skin and sinews from game or fowl. In a large soup pot, heat oil until almost smoke hot. Dredge meat cubes in flour, shaking off excess flour. Add to oil and brown. Add onions and garlic and cook until tender. Add remaining dredging flour and combine well. Add remaining ingredients. Simmer for 1 hour on low heat, uncovered.

Serve in a bowl with rice.

GAME MEATBALL SOUP

MEATBALL INGREDIENTS:
½ cup whole wheat bread crumbs (see recipe p. 172)
1 lb. ground game
½ lb. ground pork
⅓ cup Parmesan cheese
¼ cup fresh parsley, chopped
1 T. dried basil
1 tsp. garlic powder
1 tsp. onion salt
½ tsp. black pepper
½ cup flour
2 T. olive oil

SOUP INGREDIENTS:
2 cups diced onions
2 cups diced carrots
1 cup diced celery
1 qt. beef stock (see recipe p. 186)
2 bay leaves
1 tsp. thyme
2 cups whole tomatoes and juice
1 T. beef base
salt to taste
1 tsp. black pepper, freshly ground
1 cup frozen peas for garnish

Serves 4-6

HINT

Here is where you can use your imagination. Add things like mushrooms, hot or sweet peppers.

In a bowl, combine all meatball ingredients except flour and oil and make meatballs the size of walnuts. Roll meatballs in flour and brown in oil in a skillet. Remove meatballs with a slotted spoon and set aside. Add onions, carrots and celery. Cook until vegetables are tender.

Place meatballs, onions, carrots, celery, beef stock, bay leaves, thyme, tomatoes and beef base in a soup pot. Bring to a simmer and cook uncovered 40 minutes. Season with salt and pepper. Garnish with frozen peas just before serving.

CHEESEBURGER SOUP

1/4 cup olive oil
1 1/2 lbs. ground red game meat
2 cups diced onions
1 cup sliced celery
3 cloves minced garlic
2 T. all-purpose flour
4 cups beef stock (see recipe p. 186)
1 cup ketchup

1 tsp. Worcestershire sauce
2 tsp. salt
1 1/2 tsp. freshly ground black pepper
1/4 tsp. hot sauce
2 cups shredded cheddar cheese
1 cup chopped green onions
1 cup chopped dill pickles

HINT

*Add diced tomatoes
and sour cream.
Also, instead of
olive oil use 1/2 lb.
of diced bacon,
browned.*

In a large soup pot, heat oil very hot. Cook ground game meat, onions, celery and garlic. Cook until vegetables are tender and meat is brown. Stir in flour. Continue to cook on low heat for 2 minutes, stirring occasionally.

Add beef stock, ketchup, Worcestershire sauce, salt and pepper and hot sauce. Simmer for 30 minutes on low heat. Serve in bowls topped with cheese, green onions and pickles.

SPICY ANTELOPE SOUP

2 cups ground antelope meat
1 cup ground pork
2 cups cubed onions, 1/2" cubes
2 cloves garlic, minced
2 cups beef stock or game stock
(see recipe p. 186)
2 cups crushed tomatoes and juice

2 cups hot salsa
1/2 cup honey
1 jalapeño pepper, diced
2 tsp. chili powder
1 tsp. black pepper
1 tsp. salt

In a saucepan, brown antelope and pork. Add onions and garlic. Cook 5 minutes, stirring occasionally to keep from sticking. Add beef stock. Simmer for 10 minutes. Skim all fat from the top. Add remaining ingredients and simmer for 30 minutes on low. Adjust seasoning to desired taste. Serve soup with tortillas.

*This goes with all red game meat.
If you like red-hot food, add extra peppers or pepper sauce.*

Gulyassuppe (Goulash Soup)
Side dish: Sunflower Cornbread

GULYASSUPPE (GOULASH SOUP)

¼ cup clarified butter (see recipe p. 172)
1½ lbs. very lean game meat, cut into 1″ cubes
½ cup all-purpose flour
1 tsp. salt
1 tsp. coarse ground black pepper
3 cups diced onions
3 cups diced peeled celery
3 garlic cloves, crushed
2 tsp. Hungarian paprika
1 quart beef stock (see recipe p. 186)
6 cups diced tomatoes and juice
2 cups tomato purée
3 cups sliced fresh mushrooms
2 cups diced potatoes
1 T. Worcestershire sauce
sour cream for topping

Serves 6-8

HINT

Add 8 oz. of green or red bell peppers, blanched and diced ½″. Cook with mushrooms and potatoes.

Place clarified butter in a heavy soup pot and heat until almost smokey hot. Roll cubed meat in flour, shaking off excess flour. Add to butter. Add salt and pepper. Brown meat while stirring with a wooden spoon. Remove meat and set aside.

Add onions, celery and and garlic. Sauté, stirring until vegetables are transparent. Add remaining flour and stir while cooking for 2 minutes. Add cooked meat and paprika, and stir. Add beef stock, tomatoes and juice, and tomato purée and simmer slowly for 1½ hours.

Add mushrooms, potatoes and Worcestershire sauce. Simmer until potatoes are tender, but not mushy (about 30 minutes). Adjust seasoning with salt and pepper. If soup is too thick, add more beef stock to desired consistency. Serve with a dollop of sour cream.

Goulash soup is one of the great staples of Central Europe. It is also one of the heartiest and most delicious soups ever created.

Red Game Chili

Red Game Chili

1 T. olive oil
2 lbs. ground game meat
3 cups diced onions
2 cups sliced celery
2 cloves garlic, minced
3 cups diced tomatoes and juice
1 cup tomato sauce
1 cup dry red wine
1 T. beef base
1 T. chili powder
1 T. Worcestershire sauce
1 tsp. black pepper
1 tsp. red pepper flakes
1 tsp. salt
½ tsp. ground cumin
¼ tsp. ground cinnamon
3 cups canned kidney beans, drained

Serves 6-8

In a Dutch oven, heat oil over medium heat. Add meat, garlic, onions and celery. Cook until meat is brown. Add remaining ingredients, except kidney beans, and cover.

Bake in a 350° oven for 1½ hours. Add kidney beans. Combine and bake 1 hour. Adjust chili powder or red pepper flakes to taste. (This is not going to have a thick sauce.)

You may also add chili beans. For Texas style, add jalapeño peppers that have been seeded and diced.

HINT

I garnish with sour cream and shredded Swiss cheese. Top with crushed cashews.

Salads &
Sandwiches

Winged Hot Thai Salad

WINGED HOT THAI SALAD

SAUCE:
⅔ cup chicken stock (see recipe p. 186)
2 T. soy sauce
2 tsp. sesame oil
2 tsp. curry powder
1 tsp. cornstarch
¼ tsp. red pepper flakes

SALAD:
1 tsp. vegetable oil
1 cup thinly sliced onion
1 cup red pepper, sliced into ¼" strips
2 sliced serrano chili peppers or jalapeño chili peppers
½ cup carrots, sliced on bias
1 clove garlic, minced
3 cups cooked fowl, diced bite-sized
salad greens as desired
2 cups cooked white rice

Serves 4

HINT

All skin and bones should be removed from fowl before dicing.

Combine all sauce ingredients and mix well. Set aside.

In a wok or large nonstick frying pan, heat oil until smoke hot. Add onions, peppers, carrots, garlic, and sauté, to crunchy tender. (Do not overcook.)

Add meat and sauce. Cook until sauce is clear and slightly thick. Pour over salad greens and serve over white rice.

This is a great way to use leftovers.

Pheasant Kathleen Salad

PHEASANT KATHLEEN SALAD

8 large fresh strawberries, sliced
2 heads leaf or Bibb lettuce
1 cup crumbled Stilton blue cheese
¼ cup parsley
1 cup sliced peeled celery
1½ cups fresh blueberry raisins
2 tomatoes, cut into wedges
2 whole pheasant breasts
½ cup seasoned flour
1 T. olive oil
1 tsp. Worcestershire sauce
poppyseed dressing (see recipe p. 189)
freshly ground black pepper to taste

Serves 4

HINT

This works well with duck or goose breast. You may use lettuce of your choice.

To assemble salad plate: Chill 4 dinner plates. Arrange clockwise on a plate: a nest of lettuce, sliced strawberries, blueberry raisins, celery, 2 tomato wedges. Set aside.

To prepare pheasant breast: Remove skin and bones from breasts. Cut each whole breast into 8 strips the size of your little finger. Roll in flour. Shake off excess flour. Heat oil hot in a skillet and sauté pheasant fingers until done. Splash with Worcestershire sauce. Remove to a warm plate.

Place cooked pheasant fingers in lettuce nest and serve with poppyseed dressing. Garnish with freshly ground black pepper.

Southern Venison Salad

MARINADE:
⅓ cup spiced brown mustard
⅓ cup bourbon whiskey
¼ cup packed brown sugar
2 T. Worcestershire sauce
¼ tsp. hot sauce
¼ tsp. garlic powder
¼ tsp. dry mustard

4 cups venison strips
¼ cup peanut oil
1 cup cornmeal (white is best)
1 cup yellow pepper strips ¼″ × 2″ strips
1 cup red pepper strips ¼″ × 2″ strips
1 cup zucchini strips ¼″ × 2″ strips
1 cup quartered fresh mushrooms, cut in quarters
8 cups spinach leaves, stems removed

SALAD DRESSING:
1 cup red wine vinegar
¼ cup sweet and sour sauce
1 tsp. steak sauce

HINT

If you wish, you may thicken dressing with 1 T. cornstarch, cooking until liquid is clear.

Place all the marinade ingredients in a glass bowl. Combine well. Add venison strips and let stand for 24 hours in refrigerator.

Heat oil until hot in a large skillet. Remove venison from marinade. Dredge venison in cornmeal and shake off excess. Add strips to oil and brown on all sides. Set aside on a plate.

Add peppers, zucchini and mushrooms; sauté until vegetables are tender. (Do not overcook.) Add meat and ½ cup marinade. Simmer for 2 minutes.

To make dressing, combine red wine vinegar, sweet and sour sauce, and steak sauce to make a smooth dressing.

Place 2 cups fresh spinach leaves on a large platter. Top with venison-vegetable mixture and salad dressing.

This can be made with any game meat as long as all the fat and silver skin is removed.

ROAST GAME, RED CABBAGE AND
JOHN'S HORSERADISH SALAD

1 lb. cold cooked roast game, medium rare

VEGETABLE DRESSING:
⅓ cup olive oil
2 T. Dijon mustard
⅔ cup plain yogurt
1 tsp. freshly ground black pepper
1 cup sliced peeled celery
1 cup cubed fennel root, ¼" cubes
1 T. chopped fresh cilantro
½ cup John's horseradish (see recipe p. 65)

CABBAGE MIXTURE:
¼ cup olive oil
2 cups red onion strips, sliced in ¼" strips
2 cups finely shredded red cabbage
1 cup crumbled blue cheese, for garnish
1 cup pickled grapes, for garnish (see recipe p. 66)

HINT

If you don't have pickled grapes, seedless grapes work fine. You can also add a few chopped cashews.

Use lean roasted game (thin medium-rare slices of steak work even better). Cut into thin slices against the grain.

To make vegetable dressing, combine ⅓ cup olive oil, Dijon mustard, yogurt and black pepper in a bowl. Whisk until smooth. Add celery, fennel, horseradish and cilantro; combine.

To make cabbage mixture, heat ¼ cup olive oil in a large skillet. Add onion and sauté until tender. Add cabbage and sauté just until wilted (about 3 minutes). Remove from skillet and cool completely.

In a large bowl, place cabbage mixture and sliced game. Add vegetable dressing and toss gently. Place on 4 chilled plates and garnish with blue cheese and pickled grapes.

GAME CAESAR SALAD

2 heads romaine lettuce
2 cups ½" croutons
1 cup Caesar dressing
(see recipe p. 185)
½ cup shredded Parmesan cheese
⅓ cup sliced black olives

1 small red onion, sliced ¼"
thick (optional)
4 boneless fowl breasts, or
1½ lbs. red game meat
2 tsp. vegetable oil
Worcestershire sauce

Serves 4

Clean, wash and remove ribs from romaine lettuce. In a large bowl, tear romaine into bite-size pieces. Add croutons, dressing, Parmesan cheese, black olives and onions. Toss gently to combine.

For fowl, only use boneless breast and cut into pieces the size of your little finger. For red game, remove all fat, silver skin and sinews, and cut into finger size pieces.

In a heavy skillet, place vegetable oil and sauté meat strips until medium-rare. Splash with Worcestershire sauce and serve on top of salad.

PHEASANT COBB SALAD FEAST

1 head iceberg lettuce
4 cups salad greens
1½ cups cooked bacon pieces
2 cups mandarin oranges, drained
4 hard-cooked eggs, chopped
2 cups diced red tomatoes

1 cup crumbled fresh blue cheese
4 whole pheasant breasts
½ cup all-purpose flour
olive oil cooking spray
1 T. Worcestershire sauce
salad dressing of choice

Serves 4

Before cooking pheasant breast, set up salad. First make a bowl from the head of iceberg lettuce. Place lettuce bowl on a dinner plate. Combine remaining iceberg lettuce pieces with the salad greens and fill the lettuce bowl. Top with lines of bacon pieces, mandarin oranges, egg crumbles, tomato pieces and blue cheese. Set aside.

Remove skin and bones from pheasant breast. (All meat should be free of fat and silver skin.) Lightly flatten breast with meat mallet. Dredge meat in flour and shake off excess flour. Lightly coat with olive oil (I use cooking spray). Grill or pan-fry until juices run clear. Splash with Worcestershire sauce. Cut meat into strips the size of your finger. Top with pheasant fingers and serve with dressing of choice.

Kathleen, my wife, likes sliced strawberries with this also.

HINT

This salad works with all red game and fowl. If you are not a blue cheese fan, use your favorite kind of cheese.

Pheasant Breast Salad
with Grapes and Blue Cheese

2 boneless pheasant breasts
1/4 cup all-purpose flour
1/2 tsp. salt
1/2 tsp. freshly ground black pepper
1 T. vegetable oil
1 T. Worcestershire sauce

1 cup seedless green grapes
1 cup sliced peeled celery
1 cup unsalted peanuts
1 cup blue cheese dressing
1/2 cup crumbled blue cheese

HINT

To peel celery, use a potato peeler. Use your imagination and add anything you would like to the salad.

Debone, skin and cut pheasant breast into strips the size of your little finger. Dredge in flour seasoned with salt and pepper. Shake off excess flour.

Heat oil hot in a skillet. Sauté pheasant until golden brown on all sides. Add Worcestershire sauce and remove from heat. Cover.

In a bowl, combine seedless grapes, celery, peanuts and blue cheese dressing. Toss well. Add pheasant fingers and crumbled blue cheese and gently toss to combine.

Serve in a half of melon of your choice or a lettuce cup.

Elk and Wild Rice Salad

1 1/2 cups uncoated wild rice
1/2 cup mayonnaise
1/2 cup sour cream
1 T. sugar
1 T. yellow mustard
1 T. Worcestershire sauce
1/2 tsp. freshly ground black pepper

1 1/2 cups drained pineapple chunks
(or substitute seedless grapes)
1 cup cashews
1/2 cup halved water chestnuts
1 lb. elk steak, cut into strips
1/2 cup all-purpose flour
2 T. vegetable oil

Cook wild rice according to package directions. Drain well and cool.

Combine mayonnaise, sour cream, sugar, mustard, Worcestershire sauce and black pepper in a bowl. Add wild rice, pineapple, cashews and water chestnuts. Stir gently. Keep in refrigerator until ready to serve.

Remove all fat and silver skin from the elk. Cut into strips the size of your little finger. Roll strips in flour. Shake off excess flour. In a heavy skillet, add vegetable oil and heat until hot. Add the elk strips. Cook strips until brown. Turn and cook to medium rare. Place rice salad on lettuce leaves and top with warm elk strips. Serve.

BROWN BEER CRUMBLED BURGER

1 lb. ground pork	1 tsp. black pepper
1/2 lbs. ground game meat	1 tsp. ground cumin
2 cloves garlic, minced	1/2 tsp. ground coriander
1 cup diced onion	1 tsp. fennel seeds
1 cup diced celery	1/2 cup dark beer
2 tsp. salt	4-6 buns

Heat a large heavy skillet. Add ground pork, ground game and garlic. Cook until meat just starts to brown. It will look gray. Add onion, celery and spices. Stir well with a wooden spoon. Cook for 3 minutes. Add beer and stir in. Simmer on low heat for 20 minutes. When beer is evaporated, serve mixture on toasted buns with yellow mustard and ketchup.

This is almost like Sloppy Joe mix. If you wish you can use barbecue sauce instead of beer.

WILD GAME BARBECUE

2 lbs. game roast
2 cups thinly sliced onions
1 cup barbecue sauce
1/2 cup diced dill pickles, cut in 1/4" cubes
1/2 cup chili sauce
1/2 cup dry red wine
1 tsp. black pepper
8 American cheese slices
8 rye buns

Remove all fat and silver skin from meat. Place meat in a roaster pan and roast at 300° until meat has an internal temperature of 130° (medium rare). Remove from oven and let cool. Slice against the grain as thin as you can.

In a casserole, gently combine the sliced meat, onions, barbecue sauce, pickles, chili sauce, red wine and black pepper. Cover and bake for 1 hour at 350°. Serve on dark buns topped with your favorite kind of cheese.

This is great hot or cold.

This recipe is great with leftover goose or duck.

Barbecue Log Cabin Burgers

½ cup mayonnaise
¼ cup German mustard
2 small cloves garlic, minced
1 lb. ground game meat
1 lb. ground pork
1 tsp. onion salt

1 tsp. freshly ground black pepper
½ cup barbecue sauce
4 slices Swiss cheese
4 large hamburger buns
1 red pepper, sliced into 8 rings
2 cups fried onions

Makes 4 burgers

In one small bowl, combine mayonnaise, German mustard and garlic to make a sauce. In another bowl, combine ground game, ground pork, onion salt and black pepper.

Form meat into 4 large flat patties, about 1″ thick. Grill or pan-fry on medium heat. When brown on both sides, top each with 1 tablespoon barbecue sauce. Cook medium to medium well. Top each with one slice Swiss cheese and let it melt.

To serve, split bun. On top half place 2 tablespoons mayonnaise sauce, red pepper ring and ½ cup fried onions. Place burger patty on bottom half and serve with a kosher pickle spear.

HINT

The reason I add ground pork is because game is so lean. I also like to use a hard roll instead of hamburger buns.

Spicy Fried Goose Breast Sandwich

8 goose breast pieces
1 T. Worcestershire sauce
2 cloves garlic, minced
2 tsp. Hungarian paprika
1 tsp. freshly ground black pepper
1 tsp. onion powder
½ tsp. almond extract
¼ tsp. cayenne pepper

3 drops hot sauce
¼ cup peanut oil
1 cup biscuit mix
2 tsp. lemon pepper
1 T. lemon juice
4 onion bagels, toasted
½ cup cream cheese

Remove skin and all silver skin from goose breast pieces. Place pieces in a sealable bag and flatten to ½″ thickness. Combine Worcestershire sauce, garlic, paprika, black pepper, onion powder, almond extract, cayenne pepper and hot sauce. Add to goose breast and refrigerate overnight.

Heat peanut oil in a heavy skillet. Remove breast from marinade. Combine biscuit mix and lemon pepper and dredge meat in mixture. Add to hot oil and sauté until brown. Turn breast and splash with lemon juice. Cover and bake in a 350° oven for 20 minutes.

While breasts are baking, toast bagels and spread with cream cheese. Remove breast from oven. Place on top of bagels and serve.

Open-Faced Melt

OPEN-FACED MELT

4 cups leftover cooked game or fowl meat
4 slices whole grain bread, lightly toasted
4 T. Thousand Island dressing
4 tsp. horseradish
2 tomatoes, cut into ½″ slices
2 avocados, peeled and cut into ½″ slices
1 cup alfalfa sprouts
1 red onion, sliced
8 slices Monterey Jack pepper cheese, ⅛″ thick
hot peppers

Remove all bones, sinews and fat from cooked game. Slice or julienne meat into small pieces.

Toast bread lightly. Lay bread slices on a baking sheet. Top each with 1 tablespoon Thousand Island dressing, 1 tsp. horseradish, 2 slices tomato, 2 avocado slices, ⅓ cup alfalfa sprouts, 1 cup game meat, 2 onion slices and 2 slices pepper cheese.

Place in a 400° oven until cheese turns golden brown, about 10-15 minutes.

Serve with hot peppers of your choice.

HINT

If you like your cheese mild, try this recipe with your favorite cheese. It is very important to remove all sinews from meat.

GRILLED STILTON CHEESE GAME SANDWICH

1 lb. thinly sliced game roast or thinly sliced cooked game steak
1 cup Stilton cheese
¼ cup mayonnaise
1 tsp. horseradish
1 tsp. Worcestershire sauce

½ tsp. black pepper freshly ground
1 tsp. sugar
8 slices whole wheat bread
1½ cups fried onions
1 T. butter

For meat: Use roast cooked medium rare or steak broiled medium rare. Slice as thin as you can against the grain.

In a bowl, combine Stilton cheese, mayonnaise, horseradish, Worcestershire sauce, black pepper and sugar to make a paste. Lay out 8 slices bread. Evenly spread paste on slices. Top 4 slices with 4 oz. pieces of meat and remaining 4 bread slices with fried onions.

In a large skillet or on grill, melt butter. Set bread slices on griddle, filled side up. Brown to golden brown. Turn and let meat and onion heat for 1-2 minutes. Combine meat and onion slices to make sandwiches.

GAME PITA

1½ lbs. game meat
¼ cup olive oil
1 T. Worcestershire sauce
4 whole-wheat pitas, cut in half
1 head iceberg lettuce, shredded
4 cups chopped tomatoes, chopped 1" cubes
2 cups diced peeled cucumbers

2 cups diced red peppers
1 cup ranch dressing
1 cup French dressing
1 cup sliced black olives
1 tsp. salt
1 tsp. freshly ground black pepper
1½ cups crumbled feta cheese

Makes 8 pita halves

Remove all fat and silver skin from meat. Cut meat into strips the size of your little finger.

Crumble feta cheese and cut pita bread in half.

In a heavy skillet, heat oil almost smoke hot. Add game strips and brown on all sides. Splash with Worcestershire sauce and remove from heat

In the bottom of pita halves, evenly place shredded lettuce, tomatoes, cucumbers, peppers and olives. Add 2 tablespoons each of ranch and French dressings. Add hot game strips. Season with salt and black pepper. Garnish with feta cheese and more ranch and French dressing.

ITALIAN GAME STEAK

4 game steaks, 1" thick
1 8-oz. bottle Italian dressing
8 slices Italian bread
½ cup olive oil
8 provolone cheese slices
8 eggplant slices, ½" thick

4 zucchini slices, cut in half
4 onion slices, ½" thick
8 green pepper slices, ½" thick
8 fresh mushrooms, sliced ¼" thick
12 tomato slices, ¼" thick
2 tsp. dry oregano

Remove all fat and silver skin from steak. Place steak in dish and cover with Italian dressing. Let marinate in refrigerator for 3 days.

Brush Italian bread slices on both sides lightly with olive oil. Put on baking sheet. Top each with 1 slice provolone cheese. Bake at 375° until cheese starts to bubble and bread is golden brown. Remove from oven and baking sheet.

Sauté eggplant, zucchini, onion, green pepper and mushrooms in olive oil until tender. Remove vegetables to platter for assembly.

Grill steak to desired doneness. While steaks are cooking, place cheese toast on an oiled baking sheet. When steaks are cooked, place steaks on top of cheese toast. Top each with a layer of eggplant, zucchini, onion, green pepper, mushrooms and sliced tomatoes. Drizzle each with Italian dressing. Sprinkle with oregano and brown in a 375° oven until vegetables are hot.

When cooking vegetable slices, be careful to keep each vegetable intact.

HINTS

This sandwich takes some forethought. It is well worth it!

CHEESE, PHEASANT BREAST AND PEPPER SANDWICH

4 pheasant breast halves, flattened
1 cup seasoned flour (add salt and pepper)
2 T. olive oil
12 red pepper slices, ¼" thick
8 yellow pepper slices, ¼" thick

4 onion slices, ¼" thick
2 T. balsamic vinegar
1 tsp. dry thyme
4 hard onion rolls or kaiser rolls
8 dill Havarti cheese slices

Flatten pheasant breast halves to ½" thickness. Dredge in seasoned flour. Shake off excess flour. Heat olive oil in a heavy skillet. Add breast halves and brown lightly. Turn and add peppers, onion, vinegar and thyme. Cover and cook over medium heat for about 5 minutes, or until onion and peppers are just tender.

Place 1 breast half and generous amount of vegetables on bottom of roll. Top with cheese. Cover with top of roll and serve.

If you don't have balsamic vinegar, use Worcestershire sauce.

If you feel creative, add some wild mushrooms to the vegetables or top with avocado slices.

Supporting Cast

SCHUMACHER HOTEL SWEET ROLL STUFFING

12 cups cubed dry sweet rolls, doughnuts,
pastries or breads, 1" cubes
poultry parts
2 qts. water
2 cups diced onions, divided
2 cups diced celery, divided
2 bay leaves
½ cup butter
2 cloves garlic, minced

12 oz. sausage meat
2 cups chicken stock (see recipe p. 186)
1 cup eggs (about 4)
½ cup milk
1½ tsp. chicken base
2 tsp. poultry seasoning
1 tsp. dry thyme
1 tsp. dry sage
1 tsp. black pepper

Cube sweet rolls, doughnuts, pastries or breads (dark or white) of any kind into 1″ cubes.

Boil poultry parts including neck, heart, gizzard and wings with 2 quarts water, 1 cup diced onion, 1 cup chopped celery and two bay leaves. (Do not use poultry livers. Save these for pâté.) Boil until meat is tender and is ready to fall off the bone. Strain, remove poultry parts, and pick meat from wings and neck. Combine with heart and gizzard. Cool and grind. Save stock but discard bay leaves.

Melt butter to a fast bubble in a frying pan. Add remaining onions and celery. And garlic and sauté until transparent. Add sausage, cover and cook until sausage is done. Set aside to cool.

Blend remaining ingredients together with a wire whisk. Place all ingredients together in a large bowl and let sit for 20 minutes. Mix gently to combine. Be careful not to overmix or you may lose the identity of the various cubes.

Bake stuffing in a covered buttered baking dish for 2½ hours at 350°. (I recommend baking stuffing separately because fowl can carry bacteria in their cavities.)

For a Central European fruit stuffing, add ½ cup chopped apples, ½ cup chopped pears,
½ cup chopped prunes and ¼ cup raisins to the recipe.

HINT

To accumulate enough cubes for this recipe, you may cube and freeze leftover pastries. When using frozen cubes, be sure to thaw.

CHIPPEWA WILD RICE CASSEROLE

1 cup uncooked wild rice
½ lb. mushrooms sliced
½ cup sunflower seeds
3 T. minced shallots
1 bay leaf

1 tsp. Worcestershire sauce
2 cups chicken stock
(see recipe p. 186)
¼ cup butter

Rinse wild rice under running water; drain.

Combine rice, mushrooms, sunflower seeds, shallots, bay leaf and Worcestershire sauce in a 2-quart casserole. Add stock, dot with butter, cover and bake at 325° for about 1 hour, until rice is tender and liquid is absorbed. Discard bay leaf.

HINT

Wild mushrooms taste the best!

ROOT BEER CRANBERRIES

12 oz. root beer
12-oz. bag fresh or frozen cranberries

1½ cups sugar
1 T. cornstarch

Place root beer and cranberries in a saucepan and bring to a boil. Mix together sugar and cornstarch and add to saucepan. Simmer for 5 minutes, until liquid becomes clear and shiny. Chill cranberry mixture and serve. This can also be served hot.

Here is a fun idea. For 4 portions of mousse, whip 2 pints heavy whipping cream (the heavier the better) until cream is stiff. Fold in 1 cup Root Beer Cranberries. In 4 tall, stemmed glasses, layer the cream mixture with the Root Beer Cranberries to the desired fullness.

DUMPLINGS

1½ cups all-purpose flour
2 tsp. baking powder
1 tsp. salt

1 tsp. dry tarragon
¼ cup butter
¾ cup milk

In a bowl, combine flour, baking powder, salt and tarragon. Add butter and toss to make a crumbly mixture. Add milk and stir gently to make dough. Do not overmix, but make sure there are no dry flour spots. Drop into bubbling stew. Cover and simmer for 10 minutes. (Do not lift the cover, while cooking.)

KNEDLIKY (CZECH POTATO DUMPLINGS)

4 cups mashed potatoes
4 cups bread flour
1 egg, beaten
1 T. farina or Cream of Wheat
1 tsp. salt

Makes 10 dumplings

Peel, boil and mash potatoes. (It is all right to use instant mashed potatoes.) Cool.

Place cold mashed potatoes in a large bowl with flour, egg, farina and salt. Mix by hand to combine all ingredients.

When thoroughly mixed, let dough stand for five minutes. Shape in 3 oz. cylinder-shaped dumplings.

Bring a large pot of salted water to a boil and add dumplings. Dumplings will fall to the bottom of the pot, so stir them gently off the bottom. Bring back to a brisk boil for 15 minutes. Check dumpling for doneness by slicing one in half. It is done when it appears fluffy and white all the way through. Remove dumplings from water and drain. Make a slit in the center of each and brush with butter.

For fried dumplings (my favorite for breakfast), cut each dumpling into four slices, and fry them in butter until golden brown.

For stuffed dumplings, make each dumpling ⅓-cup size. Roll into a ball. Press a hole into the dumpling with your thumb. Fill the hole with stuffing and reshape, covering up the stuffing. Boil in salted water for 15-20 minutes and serve. Suggested fillings: Meat: diced ham, Canadian bacon bits, diced Polish sausage, other sausage meats and corned beef. Vegetables: diced onions, diced peppers, salted white cabbage, diced mushrooms, peas (all vegetables should be precooked). Cheese: any kind cut into small pieces. Fruit for a dessert: plums, diced apricots or diced spicy apples. Top with powdered sugar glaze.

To make 4 cups of mashed potatoes, use about 5 medium-to-large potatoes. Measure flour, don't weigh it. Always use equal amounts of mashed potatoes and flour by volume.

Baking Powder Dumplings

2 eggs, beaten
1/4 cup milk
2 T. oil or melted butter
1/2 tsp. salt

1 cup all-purpose flour
1 T. Cream of Wheat or farina
2 tsp. baking powder

Beat eggs to a froth. Add milk, oil and salt. Combine flour, cream of wheat and baking powder. Add to liquid. Gently mix to combine. Do not overmix.

With desired spoon size, dip spoon into boiling liquid (soup, water, etc.). Dip spoon into batter and dip into boiling liquid. Continue until batter is gone. Cover and simmer 12-15 minutes.

For variety add 2 teaspoons of one of the following: fresh dill, fresh herbs, Parmesan cheese, diced shallots (cooked and cooled), or 3 tablespoons shredded cheese.

Shiitake Risotto with Pine Nuts

2 cups quartered shiitake mushrooms
2 T. butter
1/2 cup diced shallots
2 cups, uncooked medium-grain white rice
4 cups chicken stock (see recipe p. 186)
1/2 cup white vermouth
1/2 tsp. white pepper
1/2 cup pine nuts
1/3 cup Parmesan cheese

Wash and remove stems from mushrooms. Cut tops into quarters and keep stems for other uses.

In a straight-sided skillet, heat butter to a fast bubble. Add shallots and cook until tender. (Do not brown.) Add rice. Stir to combine and sauté until well coated with butter. Add 2 cups chicken stock to rice. Cook over medium heat, stirring slowly until stock is absorbed and rice is almost dry. Add another cup of stock and repeat procedure. Add vermouth and white pepper. Repeat procedure. Add last cup of stock and mushrooms. Cook until rice is tender but still firm. It will appear creamy. Add nuts and Parmesan cheese. Remove from heat and gently combine.

VENISON LIVER DUMPLINGS

8 oz. venison liver
4 strips bacon, diced ½″
½ cup chopped onion
1 egg
1 T. heavy cream
1 T. lemon zest, grated fine
2 cloves garlic

⅛ tsp. ground nutmeg
⅛ tsp. ground cloves
2 cups day-old bread, crusts removed and diced in ¼″ cubes
¼ cup all-purpose flour
1 T. soft butter
1 qt. beef stock (see recipe p. 186)

Remove all membranes from liver. Place liver, bacon, onion, egg, cream, lemon zest, garlic and spices into a blender. On high speed, blend to a smooth paste.

In a mixing bowl, combine bread cubes, flour and butter. Add liver paste and mix. Dough must be firm enough to make dumplings the size of walnuts. If it is too loose, add fresh bread crumbs to tighten dough. Form dumplings.

In a large pot, heat stock to a slow rolling boil. Add dumplings and cook for 8 to 10 minutes. Remove and serve with assorted greens and wild rice.

EGG NOODLES

1¼ cups all-purpose flour
1 whole egg
5 egg yolks

2 T. melted butter
1 T. cold water
½ tsp. salt

Serves 4

Put 1 cup flour, whole egg, yolks, butter, water and salt in a bowl. Stir with a wooden spoon to make a dough. Remove to floured board.

Knead dough, working in remaining ¼ cup flour. (Do not overknead because the dough will become tough.) Cover with a cloth and let rest for 30 minutes.

Cut dough in half before rolling out. Roll out as if it were a pie crust, ¼″ thick, and cut into thin strips with a pizza cutter or sharp knife. Toss with a small amount of flour to keep noodles from sticking together. Let dry for 30 minutes.

To cook, bring 2 quarts salted water to a fast boil. Add one tablespoon butter and the noodles. Return to a boil and cook for 15-20 minutes. Drain well. Add one tablespoon butter, toss and serve.

HINTS

You may also serve dumplings with broth to make a soup. I add ¼ cup dry white wine for soup. These are great in all soups, really, and can evenly be served with barbecue sauce.

Store uncooked noodles in a tightly covered container and refrigerate. You can also freeze noodles, but don't thaw before cooking.

CLASSIC SPAETZLE

4 eggs
1/4 cup cold water
1/4 tsp. salt

1/4 tsp. ground nutmeg
1 3/4 cups all-purpose flour

HINT

If you don't have a spaetzle maker, you can make a homemade version. Press dough through a deep-fat fryer basket.

Break 4 eggs into a medium-sized bowl. Add water, salt and nutmeg. Beat with a wire whisk until frothy. Add flour slowly until the mixture is stiff and gathers around the whisk. Remove any mixture from whisk and continue stirring with a spoon until it comes off the sides of the bowl.

Bring salted water to a boil. Put dough into a spaetzle maker and drop into boiling water. Bring water back to a boil and simmer for 2 minutes. After cooking, remove spaetzle from boiling water; rinse under cold water. Drain well. Line pan with a dry cotton towel. Place spaetzle on towel and cover until ready to use.

To serve, melt butter in a skillet and sauté spaetzle, being careful not to brown. Spaetzle can also be served with pan gravy. Spaetzle will keep for about 4 days in refrigerator.

While sautéing, you can make a number of variations of this famous dish by adding chopped parsley, bacon bits, salt and nutmeg. Or sauté minced onions or shallots, add Parmesan cheese, or combine all of the above.

This dish is one of the supreme contributions of German cuisine to world cooking. It is not hard to make but it should be approached with respect and care.

SCHUMACHER HOTEL SAUERKRAUT

2 lbs. fresh or frozen sauerkraut
1/3 cup sugar
1 1/2 T. all-purpose flour
1 tsp. chicken base

1/4 tsp. white pepper
2 tsp. caraway seeds
1 1/4 cups chicken stock
(see recipe p. 186)

Serves 4

Place sauerkraut in a colander and rinse under cold water. Let drain. Mix sugar, flour, chicken base and white pepper together. Place all ingredients in a heavy pot and mix gently. Bring to a slow boil at medium heat. Stir and simmer for 15 minutes.

Sauerkraut should be made at least 2-3 hours in advance to allow flavors to fuse. Reheat and serve.

GRANDMA SCHUMACHER'S HASH BROWNS

6 cups grated raw potatoes
2 tsp. fresh lemon juice
½ cup diced onion
½ cup heavy cream
1 tsp. salt
½ tsp. white pepper
¼ cup butter

Grate or shred potatoes. Put potatoes and lemon juice in a bowl, toss gently and let sit for 10 minutes. Drain off excess liquid. Add onion, cream, salt and pepper; mix.

In a medium, nonstick frying pan, bring butter to a fast bubble. Add potato batter and cover. (Potatoes should be about 2 inches thick.) Cook over medium heat until potatoes are brown. Turn potatoes, cover, and cook until potatoes are light brown on both sides. Remove from pan and cut into squares.

If using an electric frying pan, cut potato cake in quarters before turning.
Be careful not to use too large a frying pan.

SKILLET CAMP POTATOES

6 cups sliced potatoes, unpeeled
1 cup sliced onion
⅓ cup butter, melted
2 tsp. garlic salt
¼ tsp. black pepper

½ cup shredded sharp cheddar cheese
1 cup chicken stock (see recipe p. 186)
1 tsp. Worcestershire sauce
¼ cup barbecue sauce

Wash and slice potatoes. Cut onions in half, then slice into ¼″ strips.

Line a baking pan or skillet with double thickness of foil to create a foil pan. Combine potatoes, onion, butter, and salt and pepper. Place in pan. Top with cheese. Add chicken stock and Worcestershire sauce. Remove foil pan from baking pan and grill over medium heat for 35-40 minutes, or until potatoes are tender. Sprinkle with barbecue sauce and serve.

HINT

The reason we use the double-thick foil is to create the shape. Roll the edges of the foil for strength. Potatoes should be cooked uncovered.

STUFFED SWEET POTATOES

4 sweet potatoes   *2 T. butter, softened*
8 strips bacon, diced   *1 tsp. salt*
1 cup diced onion   *1 tsp. ground nutmeg*
½ cup sour cream   *⅓ cup chopped pecans*

Wash and bake sweet potatoes in a 375° oven for 50 minutes, or just until tender when pinched. Let potatoes cool enough to be handled.

While potatoes are baking, dice and brown bacon. When bacon is brown, add onions and cook until tender. Remove to strainer and strain bacon grease by pressing gently on mixture.

Lay potatoes on side and slice ½″ off top. Remove pulp from top and inside of potato, leaving a ¼″ thick wall.

In a bowl, combine pulp, sour cream and butter. Mash with potato masher. Add bacon, onion, salt and nutmeg. Combine well. Stuff potatoes with equal amounts of filling. Sprinkle pecans on top.

To serve, heat oven to 350°. Bake potatoes for 20-25 minutes, or until heated through.

SUN-DRIED TOMATOES

PEPPER RUB:
¼ cup olive oil
1 T. freshly cracked black pepper
1 T. coarse salt
1 T. minced garlic

10 ripe baseball-sized tomatoes, stemmed and halved

In a large bowl, combine all pepper rub ingredients. Add tomatoes and toss gently to combine. Arrange the tomato halves in a single layer on top of a rack placed in a large baking sheet. Bake in a 180° oven overnight, or about 12 hours. As they cook, the tomatoes will become wrinkled and shrink. After 12 hours, remove the tomatoes and set them aside to cool.

Store in a tightly covered glass container or in olive oil, and refrigerate.

Replace a small piece of potato plug on each end to seal potatoes. If you wish, you can add additional barbecue sauce to the outside of the potato before closing foil.

BARBECUE-STUFFED CAMPFIRE POTATOES

4 large Idaho baking potatoes
1 cup shredded farmer cheese
½ cup barbecue sauce
1 tsp. onion salt
½ tsp. black pepper

Serves 4

Wash potatoes. With an apple corer, remove a plug lengthwise from the center of potatoes. In a bowl, combine shredded cheese, barbecue sauce, onion salt and black pepper. Evenly stuff center of potatoes.

Wrap potatoes tightly in a double thickness of aluminum foil. Bake on campfire or grill until potatoes are tender when pressed. You can bake the potato in a 375° oven for 1 hour. Remove from foil and serve with sour cream.

ROSTI POTATOES

1 ½ lbs. potatoes
8 oz. Swiss cheese
1 tsp. salt
pinch of white pepper

Serves 4

Boil potatoes until tender and drain immediately. Cool and peel. Shred into a bowl. Shred Swiss cheese into same bowl. Add salt and pepper, and mix well. Fry in a hot buttered cast iron skillet or nonstick pan. Brown on one side and turn. Serve directly from skillet to table.

SCHUMACHER HOTEL RED CABBAGE

1 head red cabbage (about 3½ lbs.)
¼ lb. bacon, chopped
1½ cups thinly sliced onions
¾ cup apple juice
½ cup red wine vinegar
½ tsp. black pepper
2 fresh garlic cloves, minced
1 T. beef base
2 T. brown sugar
½ cup dry red wine
1 red apple, peeled and chopped

Serves 8

Core and cut cabbage into quarters. Thinly slice each quarter. In a stock pot, sauté until brown and crisp. Add onion and cook until clear and tender.

Add cabbage and remaining ingredients, except apples. Stir well, making sure nothing is sticking to bottom of pot. Cover and cook on low heat for 30 minutes, stirring gently and often. Add apples and cook for 15 minutes more.

This is one of the classic accompaniments of German
and Central European cuisine.

It is best to make this dish 1-2 days in advance and store it in the refrigerator until you use it. It is easy to prepare and can be stored in your refrigerator for up to a week.

Morel Mushroom Sauté

6-8 large fresh morel mushrooms
salt and pepper to taste
½ cup seasoned flour (add salt and pepper)
2 T. butter
2 T. lemon juice
1 T. dry white wine

Serves 4

Wash and slice morel mushrooms in half. Season with salt and pepper. Dust with flour. Heat butter in a frying pan to a fast bubble. Add mushrooms and sauté for about 20 seconds. Turn and sauté 20 more seconds. Add lemon juice and wine and sauté another 30 seconds.

Serve immediately.

Roasted Garlic

4 bulbs garlic
⅓ cup olive oil
1 tsp. dry rosemary
1 tsp. dry thyme
¼ tsp. salt
¼ tsp. fresh ground pepper

To prepare: Slice ⅛″ off the top ends of garlic bulbs. Place a double-thick sheet of foil flat on the counter. Place garlic bulbs cut end up in the center of the foil. Turn edges of foil up to start making a bundle. Top garlic with oil, spices, salt and pepper. Close up bundle and bake at 325° for 2 hours.

Serve with fresh bread and all kinds of game.

HINT

This is the best way to use garlic. Once you try this recipe, you will be spoiled for life.

CHEF JOHN'S HORSERADISH

5 cups shredded fresh horseradish
1½ cups white wine vinegar
½ cup cold water
½ cup sugar
½ tsp. white pepper
1 jalapeño pepper, sliced

Wash and peel horseradish roots with a potato peeler. Shred in a bowl. (You can chop in a food processor or grind horseradish if you wish.) Add vinegar, water, sugar and white pepper and combine well. Remove seeds and stem from jalapeño. Slice into pieces and add to horseradish mixture. Place in a covered container. (Make sure to keep this covered in the refrigerator!) Let stand for 3 days and stir. Use and enjoy.

To make horseradish hotter, add more white pepper
and another jalapeño pepper.

SOUPY CAMPBELL BEANS

1 15-oz. can kidney beans, drained
1 15.5-oz can butter beans, drained
2 15-oz. cans pork and beans
1 cup packed brown sugar
1¼ cups coarsely chopped onions
½ cup ketchup
2 tsp. yellow mustard
⅓ cup dill pickle juice
¼ cup maple syrup

Place all ingredients into a heavy pot. Simmer, uncovered, on low heat for 45 minutes, or until onions are tender, stirring gently to keep from sticking.

You can also add ground game. Soupy Campbell and I were submarine sailors together.

HINT

For my kids, I brown 2 lbs. ground venison, drain the fat and add it to the beans. My family calls this "Slumgovia."

PICKLED GRAPES WITH GINGER

3 cups white vinegar
2 cups white sugar
1 cup packed brown sugar
3 T. crushed coriander seeds
2 T. ground cinnamon
14 whole cloves
2 tsp. salt
½ cup diced peeled fresh ginger
1 red or green jalapeño pepper, thinly diced, with seeds
2 qts. red and/or green seedless grapes

In a large saucepan, combine the vinegar, white and brown sugars, coriander seeds, cinnamon, cloves and salt. Mix well and bring to a boil over moderately high heat. Remove from heat. Add the ginger, jalapeño peppers and grapes. Mix thoroughly and allow to stand 1 hour.

These grapes will keep indefinitely if covered and refrigerated.

HONEY SUNFLOWER CORNBREAD

1 cup half-and-half
2 large eggs, beaten
¼ cup honey
¼ cup vegetable oil
¼ cup packed brown sugar
½ tsp. salt
1 cup all-purpose flour
1 cup yellow cornmeal
1 T. baking powder
½ cup unsalted sunflower seeds

In a bowl, combine half-and-half, eggs, honey, vegetable oil, brown sugar and salt. Whisk to a froth. Combine flour, cornmeal, baking powder and sunflower seeds. Stir dry ingredients into wet ingredients just until combined and moistened. Pour into greased 9″ square baking pan. Bake at 375° for 20 to 25 minutes, or until 1 toothpick inserted in center comes out clean.

Eat with tons of butter and honey.

HINT

If you aren't a sunflower seed fan, just substitute your favorite nuts or leave out the nuts altogether.

BLUE CHEESE SHALLOT BUTTER

1 cup softened butter, divided
¼ cup diced shallots
½ tsp. garlic powder
⅓ cup crumbled blue cheese
½ tsp. grated lemon zest
3 drops Tabasco sauce
1 pinch white pepper
1 tsp. chopped parsley

Heat ¼ cup butter in a small saucepan. Add shallots and cook until shallots are tender. Let cool. Place all ingredients in a bowl, and combine well with a large spoon. Butter should be the consistency of mayonnaise. Spoon onto a sheet of plastic wrap. Roll mixture up into 2 logs and chill. Cut off desired amount.

This can be frozen and used from a frozen state. I use this on grilled red game steaks and upland birds. This is also outstanding on fish.

BLUE PLUM PRUNE MARMALADE

1 T. olive oil
1 cup minced onion
1 clove garlic, minced
2 cups chopped stewed prunes
2 cups purple plums, pitted and quartered
1½ cups plum liquid
1 cup orange marmalade
⅓ cup port wine
2 tsp. cornstarch

In a saucepan, heat oil and sauté onion and garlic until tender. Add prunes, plums, plum liquid and marmalade. Simmer for 20 minutes on low heat. Combine cornstarch and port wine and add to sauce. Simmer until cornstarch is clear, about 8 minutes.

Serve with fowl or upland game.

HINT

If you don't have port wine, sherry will do, but remember that the sauce will have a different flavor.

CRISPY GRITS GATEAU

1 T. butter
½ cup minced shallots
2 cups chicken stock, divided
1 tsp. chicken base
9 oz. instant grits
½ cup heavy cream
⅓ cup Parmesan cheese
clarified butter (see recipe p. 172)

In a heavy saucepan, heat butter to a fast bubble. Add shallots and cook until clear. Add 1 cup chicken stock and the chicken base. Bring to a boil and simmer for 5 minutes. Remove mixture to a blender and purée until smooth. Return to pot and combine with remaining stock. Bring to a fast boil. Add grits and cook until thick, stirring with a wooden spoon.

Add cream and cheese. Cook for 5 minutes and continue stirring. Remove from heat and let cool, covered with a clean cotton towel. Roll mixture to ½″ thickness. Cut with a cookie cutter to desired shape. Heat a skillet with clarified butter. Add grits. Brown pieces on both sides. Serve.

GOURMET LEMONADE

zest of two lemons
2 cups sugar (vanilla bean sugar)
1 cup fresh-squeezed lemon juice

Remove yellow zest from lemons with a potato peeler. Combine sugar, lemon juice and zest in a heavy saucepan. Bring to a boil over medium heat. Boil for 3 minutes. Remove from heat and let cool in pan.

Keep base in container in refrigerator. To make lemonade, use 2 tablespoons base for 8 ounces cold water in a tall glass. Stir well. Add ice and stir.

I combine equal amounts of fresh lemon juice and water
and place it in ice cube trays and freeze. When frozen, I place them in a plastic bag.
Add one cube per glass of lemonade.

HINT

To make the vanilla bean sugar I put a vanilla bean split in half in a glass jar with 2 cups sugar for one week. Sometimes I like to add two vanilla beans.

SWEET CREAM BISCUITS

3 cups sifted all-purpose flour
1 T. sugar
1 T. baking powder
1 tsp. salt
1 cup milk
1 cup heavy cream
2 T. butter

In a large bowl, combine flour, sugar, baking powder and salt. Add milk, cream and butter. Stir with large spoon to combine. Turn out onto floured baking cloth. Knead 10 times, gently.

Roll or pat dough 1″-1½″ thick. Cut with a round cutter or cut into 3″ squares.

Arrange on ungreased pan so biscuits are barely touching. Bake at 400° for 15-20 minutes, or until golden brown.

OUTRAGEOUS RICE PUDDING

1 quart half-and-half
¾ cup uncooked long grain rice
1 piece lemon peel the size of your little finger
¾ cups sugar
2 egg yolks
½ cup heavy cream
½ tsp. vanilla extract
cinnamon to taste

Place half-and-half, rice and lemon peel in a heavy saucepan and cook on low heat for 1 hour, uncovered. Stir often with a wooden spoon to keep from sticking.

In a blender combine cream, sugar and yolks. Add some hot half-and-half from the pot to cream mixture. Combine and slowly add to rice.

Cook on low just until mixture comes to a slow bubble. Remove from heat and place in a container. Add vanilla and cover with plastic wrap. Punch holes in wrap to let steam out. Chill in refrigerator.

Upland Fare

Barbecued Partridge Bundles

BARBECUED PARTRIDGE BUNDLES

4 partridge or chickens
2 onions, diced 1/2"
1 1/2 cups barbecue sauce
1 tsp. salt
1 tsp. black pepper
8 bacon slices
1 head lettuce

HINT

Be careful when you turn the bundles so as not to let the liquid pour out.

Clean birds and soak in salted water for 1 hour.

Dice onions and combine with 1/2 cup barbecue sauce, and salt and pepper. Place equal amounts in cavity of each bird. Wrap 2 slices of bacon around each bird. Remove 4 large lettuce leaves and fold around birds to make a blanket. In center of double-thick foil sheet, place a partridge. Cover each with 1/4 cup barbecue sauce and fold foil around the birds, crimping tightly on top.

Bake bundles at 375° for 1 hour 15 minutes. Remove from oven and let stand for 10 minutes. Serve.

You may also cook these on a grill or over a camp fire.

BROWN TURKEY HASH

6 cups diced leftover turkey
1/3 cup butter, divided
1 1/2 cup diced red onions
1/2 cup diced red pepper
1 cup diced cooked potatoes

1/2 cup mayonnaise
1 T. tomato purée
1 tsp. paprika
1 tsp. garlic salt
1/2 tsp. freshly ground black pepper

Dice light and dark turkey meat. Remove all bones and sinews. Heat 1 tablespoon butter in a sauté pan. Add onions and red pepper and sauté until tender. Cool. In a large bowl, gently combine all ingredients, except remaining butter. In a heavy skillet, heat remaining butter to a fast bubble. Add hash mixture. Pack it firmly on the bottom and sides of skillet.

Cover and bake in oven at 375° for 20 minutes. Turn out onto a heated plate. Serve with poached eggs or tomato sauce.

Roast Pheasant with Vanilla Brandy Sauce

Roast Pheasant with Vanilla Brandy Sauce

2 pheasants, cut in half
1 cup all-purpose flour
1 cup vegetable oil
2 cups sliced mushrooms
1 cup diced shallots
1 cup chicken stock (see recipe p. 186)
1 tsp. chicken base
½ gallon vanilla ice cream
¼ cup brandy

Cut pheasants in half. Remove excess skin. Dredge meat in flour. Shake off excess flour. Heat oil hot in a heavy skillet. Add pheasant pieces and brown. Remove pheasant to a Dutch oven. Pour off all fat, except for 1 tablespoon. Add mushrooms and shallots and sauté until tender. Add to pheasant. Add chicken stock and base to pheasant. Cover and bake in a 350° oven for 1½ hours, checking to see if more liquid is needed. If so, add 1 cup of water.

Let ice cream melt in a bowl at room temperature. Add melted ice cream and brandy to pheasant. Cover and bake 1 hour longer until sauce is thick and pheasant is tender.

Sage Hen Breast with Salsa and Green Onions

6 sage hen breast pieces
1 cup shredded Parmesan cheese
1½ T. olive oil
2 cups salsa
1 cup dry red wine
1 cup sliced green onions
nacho chips

Remove skin and silver skin from birds. Cut breast pieces in half. Roll pieces in Parmesan cheese. In a skillet, heat oil until hot. Add breast pieces and cook to a golden brown on both sides. Place in casserole. Cover with salsa and red wine. Bake, covered, at 350° for 1½ hours. Add green onions. Bake for 20 minutes. Test for doneness. Serve with nacho chips.

Hint

Sage hens are very red in color and very firm in texture, so cook them slow and long. This recipe is also great with duck or goose breast.

PHEASANT À LA CREME

1 pheasant (3-3½ lbs.) cut
into quarters
1½ cups seasoned flour
(add salt and pepper)
1 cup vegetable oil
1 cup chicken stock (see recipe p. 186)

2 T. minced shallots
1½ pts. heavy cream
3 oz. (6T.) cream sherry
3 oz. (6T.) dry white wine
1 tsp. salt
salt and pepper to taste

Serves 2

Roll pheasant in flour and brown in skillet in hot oil. Drain.

Place pheasant in a casserole dish. Add chicken stock and shallots. Cover and bake at 350° for 1½ hours. Add cream, sherry, white wine and 1 teaspoon salt. Continue baking until pheasant is tender and sauce is thick, about 1½ hours. (You must use cream to get the sauce to thicken. Do not substitute.) Season to taste with salt and pepper.

This recipe is the one I grew up with. My mother still makes the best in the universe.

ROAST WILD TURKEY

1 cleaned turkey
2 tsp. salt
1 tsp. black pepper
2 large onions, peeled

1 lemon, cut in half
1 large roasting bag
1 cup dry white wine

Clean turkey and rinse cavity well. Season cavity with salt and pepper, and place onions and lemon in cavity. Do not season outside of bird, as it will make it dry. Place bird in roasting bag. Add wine to bag, seal bag and place in roasting pan. Roast at 300° for 2-3 hours. (Times will vary since each bird is different because of age, sex and weight.) Place a thermometer in the thickest part of the breast. Bake to internal temperature of 180°.

Remove turkey from bag and serve immediately. Time is very important, as the bird has no fat and will dry out quickly. The legs are full of tendons so try not to serve them.

HINT

The secret to cooking moist, tender pheasant is to cook it in chicken stock, covered, over moderate heat for a long period of time. Rabbit can be prepared this way too.

HUNGARIAN PHEASANT

2 pheasants, cut in 6 pieces
½ cup flour
⅓ cup olive oil
1½ cups dry red wine
1½ tsp. beef base
1 tsp. salt
1 cup water
2 cups diced onions
3 cloves garlic, minced
1 cup diced red peppers
½ cup diced green peppers
1 tsp. freshly ground black pepper
1½ T. Hungarian paprika
2 tsp. chopped parsley
1 cup sliced mushrooms
½ cup black olives, cut in half
1 cup sour cream for garnish

Cut pheasant into 6 pieces removing backbone. Do not use legs or wings as they are too full of sinews. Dredge pheasant in flour. Heat oil hot in a Dutch oven. Add pheasant and brown well on both sides. Pour off oil and keep for cooking the vegetables. Add red wine, beef base, salt and water. Cover and bake for 1½ hours in a 350˚ oven.

In a large sauté pan, reheat oil. Add onions, garlic and peppers. Cook until onions are tender. Add cooked vegetables, spices, mushrooms and olives to pheasant. Cover and bake 45 minutes. Serve with a large dollop of sour cream.

HINT

Mix paprika in ¼ cup hot water to make a smooth paste to keep it from lumping. I use a beef base in this recipe to give it a deeper, richer flavor. The wings, legs and backbone can be cooked to make a stock to be used later.

This recipe works well with short tails, grouse, hens, ducks or geese. Chicken can also be used. If you use chicken, you may use the legs.

Lick Your Lemon Pheasant Fingers

LICK YOUR LEMON PHEASANT FINGERS

4 boneless, skinless pheasant breasts
8 eggs
3/4 cup Parmesan cheese
1/3 cup clarified butter (see recipe p. 172)
1 cup seasoned flour (add salt and pepper)
2 cups bread crumbs (see recipe p. 172)
1 T. fresh lemon juice
2 tsp. lemon pepper seasoning

Serves 4

Remove skin and silver skin from pheasant breasts and slice each breast into 6 strips about the size of a forefinger. Combine eggs and Parmesan cheese, and beat to a smooth consistency. Heat butter in a large sauté pan. Dredge pheasant fingers in flour, dip into egg batter, and roll in bread crumbs. Sauté fingers in butter until golden brown. Splash with lemon juice and sprinkle with lemon pepper. Turn down heat and cook for 3 minutes, turning fingers over to keep from over browning.

HINTS

You can serve the fingers with assorted sauces.

BRONZED CAJUN CREAM PHEASANT BREASTS

4 boneless skinless pheasant   *2 T. currant jelly*
breasts   *1 T. cornstarch*
1 1/2 T. Cajun spices   *1 tsp. salt*
1 T. olive oil   *3 drops hot sauce*
1 1/2 cups vanilla ice cream   *2 T. horseradish*

Remove skin from pheasant breasts. Rub breasts with Cajun seasoning on both sides. Sprinkle with olive oil and place in a plastic bag for at least 1 hour.

To make the sauce, melt the ice cream in a heavy saucepan over low heat. Combine currant jelly, cornstarch, salt and hot sauce to make a smooth paste. Add to ice cream and turn heat to medium. Stirring slowly, cook until sauce is thick and just comes to a bubble. Remove from heat and add horseradish. In a heavy skillet or on the grill, cook pheasant to a bronzed brown on each side.

To serve: Place a 1/2 cup sauce in the center of the plate.
Top with a pheasant breast.

This recipe also works well with chicken breast, turkey tenderloins, or even pork cutlets. Bronzing is cooking to a dark brown but not blackened color. It keeps the flavor from becoming bitter.

Wild Cherry Breast
of Pheasant

WILD CHERRY BREAST OF PHEASANT

4 boneless, skinless pheasant breasts
(6-8 oz. each)
1½ cups seasoned flour (add salt and pepper)
¼ cup clarified butter (see recipe p. 172)
2 cups brown sauce (see recipe p. 173)
¾ cup wild cherry jam
½ cup diced shallots
½ cup dry sherry
1 T. fresh lemon juice
¼ tsp. salt
1 T. chopped fresh parsley

Serves 4

HINT

If you can't obtain wild cherry jam or preserves, use wild cherry jelly and add ½ cup unsweetened and pitted red cherries.

Clean bird and remove breast. Cut breast in half and remove skin. Lightly flatten breast halves with a meat mallet to thickness of about ¾″. Dredge in seasoned flour.

Heat butter to a fast bubble and sauté breast pieces to a golden brown on each side. Add brown sauce, wild cherry jam, shallots, sherry, lemon juice and salt. Cover and bake in a 350° oven for 45 minutes.

When serving, place 2 pheasant pieces on each plate. Top with ½ cup sauce. Garnish with chopped parsley.

PHEASANT IN A RED SEA BAG

2 pheasant breasts, split in half
2 tsp. Cajun seasoning
4 slices provolone cheese
4 slices ham, 1/8" thick
4 red peppers
1 T. olive oil

1 cup sliced red onion
1 cup chicken stock
(see recipe p. 186)
1 cup diced carrots
1 green pepper, diced 1/2"

Serves 4 for lunch

Remove breasts from pheasants. Cut breasts in half. Lay breasts between 2 plastic bags. Gently flatten with a meat mallet to about 1/2". Sprinkle each half with 1/2 teaspoon Cajun seasoning and top with a slice of provolone cheese and ham. Roll up into cylinders. Set aside.

Remove the tops of the red peppers. Remove seeds. Place 1/2 teaspoon olive oil inside. Place 1 pheasant breast cylinder in each red pepper. In between cylinder and pepper, put red onion slices to fill pepper. Top with chicken stock.

Place remaining onion slices, carrots and green pepper on bottom of casserole dish. Place filled red peppers on top. Cover and bake at 350° for 1½ hours. When meat is tender to a fork, remove from oven. Serve with vegetables and juice.

HINT

These are also very good served cold for lunch. Serve with a hard roll.

PHEASANT HIPS STROGANOFF

2 cups diced pheasant thigh meat
2 cups ground pork
1 cup fresh rye bread crumbs (see recipe p. 172)
1 egg, beaten slightly
1 T. chopped fresh parsley
1 tsp. salt
1 tsp. freshly ground black pepper
1/2 tsp. tarragon
1/2 tsp. onion powder
1 T. olive oil
1 cup quartered fresh mushrooms
2 10 1/2-oz. cans cream of mushroom soup
8 oz. half-and-half
1/2 cup sour cream
1/4 cup sherry

Serves 4

HINT

White bread crumbs work if you don't have rye bread. If you have a grinder, grind pheasant thigh meat instead of dicing it fine.

Remove skin, bones and sinews from thighs and dice thighs as fine as you can. In a bowl, place pheasant, pork, rye bread crumbs, egg, parsley, salt, pepper, tarragon and onion powder. Combine well and make meatballs the size of walnuts.

In a large skillet, heat olive oil. Add meatballs and brown on all sides over medium heat. Add mushrooms. Cover and cook 2 minutes over low heat. In a bowl, whisk the mushroom soup, half-and-half, sour cream and sherry. Add to meatballs. Simmer for 10 minutes, and serve with pasta, wild rice or white rice.

Of course, this works well with both white and dark meat. But this is a great way to use up the dark meat. Do not try to use leg meat as it has too many sinews and tendons. Frozen meat grinds better, so just place pieces in the freezer for 20 minutes.

Walnut Pheasant Breast
with Strawberry Salsa

WALNUT PHEASANT BREAST WITH STRAWBERRY SALSA

4 boneless, skinless, pheasant breasts

MARINADE:
1 cup apple juice
½ cup diced onion
¼ cup lemon juice
1 tsp. grated lemon zest
1 tsp. garlic, minced
1 tsp. freshly ground black pepper

CRUST:
¼ cup olive oil
2 cups walnut pieces
1½ cups minced onions
1 T. garlic, minced fine
1 cup whole wheat bread crumbs (see recipe p. 172)
2 T. soy sauce
2 tsp. finely chopped fresh basil
¼ cup liquid from marinade
1 cup flour
strawberry salsa (see recipe p. 183)

HINT

It is a must to use fresh bread crumbs. These pheasant breasts taste great as a cold sandwich with hot peppers or dill pickles.

Clean, skin and remove bones from pheasant breast. Flatten breast to ½″ thickness with a meat mallet. Combine all marinade ingredients in a glass bowl. Add breasts and cover. Refrigerate for 3 days, mixing once a day to evenly marinade meat.

Heat olive oil in a skillet. Add walnuts, onions and garlic. Sauté over medium heat until onions are tender. Remove from heat. Add bread crumbs, soy sauce and basil. Toss. Add ¼ cup marinade liquid. Combine to make a paste.

Remove breasts from marinade. Dredge in flour. Dip back in marinade liquid and press in crumb paste to evenly coat breasts. Place on a lightly oiled sheet pan. Bake at 350° for 45 minutes. Breasts are done when touched with a fork and the juices run clear. Remove from pan to a warm place and serve with strawberry salsa.

Sunday Night Pheasant Breast Pizza

SUNDAY NIGHT PHEASANT BREAST PIZZA

4 boneless, skinless pheasant breasts
1 tsp. garlic salt
1 tsp. freshly ground black pepper
1 cup all-purpose flour
2 T. olive oil
2 large red onions, cut into ½″ inch slices
2 large zucchini, cut into 4″ × ½″ slices
4 large fresh mushrooms, cut into ¼″ slices
2 cups pizza sauce
2 tomatoes, cut into ¼″ slices
1 tsp. dry oregano
2 tsp. basil (fresh is best)
1½ cups mozzarella cheese

Remove skin from pheasant breasts. Place breasts, one at a time, in a plastic bag. Flatten with a meat mallet to about ¼″. Season with garlic salt and pepper. Dredge in flour and shake off excess.

In a large skillet, heat 1 tablespoon olive oil. Add red onion slices and cook until tender. Remove to a plate. Add zucchini and mushrooms and cook to almost tender, but still crisp. Remove from pan. Add remaining olive oil and pheasant breasts. Sauté until both sides are a light golden brown.

Remove breasts to an oiled baking sheet. On top of each breast, place 1 tablespoon pizza sauce, 1 onion slice, 2 slices tomato, 2 zucchini strips and mushroom slices. Top with 2 tablespoons pizza sauce, spices and a generous amount of mozzarella cheese. Bake at 375° for 20 minutes and serve.

Grilled Wild Turkey

GRILLED WILD TURKEY

1 wild turkey, skinned
2 cups herb dressing
2 cups sliced onions
½ cup dry white wine
3 cloves garlic, minced
1 T. fresh lemon juice
3 bay leaves

Serves 4

After skinning turkey, wash and clean well. Set bird breast-side-up. Remove the 2 breast slabs by cutting next to the breast bone and removing the breasts in 2 large pieces. Remove the thigh and leg in 1 piece on each side. Lay thigh-leg on a cutting board, inside up. Cut off the leg at the first joint, leaving thigh. Remove the bone from the thigh. This will give you a good piece of dark meat.

Place turkey breast pieces and thigh pieces in a stainless steel bowl or glass dish. Top with herb dressing, onions, wine, garlic, lemon juice and bay leaves to make a marinade. Cover tightly and refrigerate for 3 days.

To grill, remove turkey pieces from bowl or dish, and place on grill. Baste often with marinade and grill until done. Be careful not to overcook.

Place cooked turkey pieces on a cutting board and slice thinly at an angle. Serve with hollandaise or mushroom sauce, or my personal favorite, béarnaise sauce.

HINT

Since the turkey legs are not good for this recipe, save them for soup. You can also use this recipe with domestic turkey under 15 lbs.

Quail Helenka

QUAIL HELENKA

8 quail
salt and pepper to taste
16 blue prunes
16 strips bacon
4 cups brown sauce (see recipe p. 173)
4 cups Hotel Stuffing (see recipe p. 54)

Serves 4

Wash quail and season cavities with salt and pepper. Stuff 2 blue prunes in each and wrap 1 bacon strip over the top. Wrap 1 bacon strip around each quail. Bake at 375° for 40 minutes. Place ¼ cup brown sauce or gravy on small mound of stuffing and place 1 quail on top. Repeat for other quail.

This is an elegant and wonderful dish. It is named for my mother,
who is the original inspiration for my cooking.

WHITE PEPPERCORN GRILLED QUAIL

8 quail, split
¼ cup white peppercorns
2 T. olive oil
1 T. Worcestershire sauce
1 tsp. chopped fresh tarragon

Serves 4

Clean quail. Cut through backbone and flatten bird. Place peppercorns in a plastic bag and crack with a mallet or rolling pin. Place quail in bag and shake well to coat. Let stand about 1 hour.

Heat olive oil in a large skillet. Place 4 quail, bone-side-down, in skillet and brown well. Reduce heat to low. Cover and cook 5 minutes. Remove cover. Splash with Worcestershire sauce. Remove quail to sheet pan. Keep in a 200° oven while the rest cook. When all quail are done, place on a serving plate and sprinkle with fresh tarragon leaves.

HINTS

You may also use squab for this recipe.

If birds have been skinned, it works just fine. Dove breasts and wood ducks also work well.

ENDLESSLY EASY BONELESS BREAST OF PHEASANT

4 boneless pheasant breasts
6 eggs
¾ cup Parmesan cheese
2 T. fresh lemon juice
1 cup seasoned flour (add salt and pepper)
¼ cup clarified butter (see recipe p. 172)
8 lemon slices, ¼" thick

Serves 4

This recipe is simple to make and it comes with three variations, so you can prepare it frequently.

Remove skin from boneless pheasant breasts. In a bowl, combine eggs and Parmesan cheese and whip smooth with wire whisk. The resulting batter should have a medium consistency.

Place seasoned flour in a pie plate. Heat butter in a large, heavy sauté pan. One at a time, dredge pheasant breasts in flour, then dip in Parmesan/egg mixture, coating well and dipping back into flour.

Place breasts in sauté pan. Brown lightly, turn each breast and splash with lemon juice. Place breasts in a covered casserole and bake in oven at 350° for 40 minutes. Remove and serve each with 2 lemon slices as garnish.

My own variation of this recipe is to place 1½ tablespoons of Roquefort or blue cheese on top of each pheasant breast before placing in oven.

HINT

For a hunter's style variation, top pheasant with ½ cup mushroom sauce after baking.

TOUGH GUYS CAYENNE GRILLED DOVES

16 dove breasts
1 cup hot pepper sauce
1 cup cold coffee
½ cup lime juice
½ cup chopped cilantro
1 T. molasses
2 cloves of garlic, minced
1 tsp. salt

Serves 4

Remove breast from doves. Skin and flatten breasts. If you can, remove all bones. Combine all ingredients and marinate overnight. Remove breasts from marinade. Spray with oil and grill over medium heat.
Serve with Pineapple Ginger Chutney (see recipe p. 179).

ROASTED PHEASANT

2 pheasants
1 tsp. salt
2 cups cubed onions, 1" cubes
1 lemon, cut into 8 pieces
1 tsp. black pepper
1 tsp. dry thyme
8 strips bacon
1 large roasting bag

Clean birds well and soak in 1 gallon water mixed with 1 tablespoon salt for 1 hour to remove blood. Rinse well.
Combine onions, lemon and spices and place half in each bird cavity. Place 4 strips bacon over the tops of each bird. Place pheasants in a roasting bag and roast at 250° for 3 hours. Test for doneness by placing a meat thermometer in the thickest part of the breast. Birds should be cooked to 180° internal temperature.

At 180°, the juices should run clear and the legs should separate from the body easily.

Do not have heat too high or you will blacken the breasts before they are cooked thoroughly.

Roasting pheasant is very hard as pheasants are low in fat and dry out easily. That is why we cover them with bacon.

HINT

When dredging in flour, shake off excess, but leave a small amount to slightly thicken sauce.

LEMON OSTRICH

1 lb. ostrich meat, cut into 12 thin slices
½ cup seasoned flour (add salt and pepper)
1 T. cup clarified butter (see recipe p. 172)
¼ cup minced shallots
1 cup dry white wine
½ cup brown sauce (see recipe p. 173) or gravy
2 tsp. fresh lemon juice
½ tsp. freshly ground black pepper
1½ tsp. parsley flakes
1 tsp. salt
4 lemon slices, ¼" thick
parsley sprigs

Flatten ostrich slices with a mallet. Dredge in seasoned flour. Heat clarified butter and sauté shallots until tender and clear. (Be careful not to brown.) Add ostrich slices and sauté 30 seconds. Turn and sauté 30 seconds on other side. Add wine, brown sauce, lemon juice and pepper. Simmer for 5 minutes on low heat. Add parsley and salt, and simmer for 2 minutes.

Serve 3 ostrich slices on a plate with ¼ cup sauce. Garnish with a halved lemon slice, placed on the side of the plate with a parsley sprig.

This dish should be served immediately after preparation. You may add 2 cups sliced fresh mushrooms after sautéing ostrich meat and before simmering.

Roasted Partridge Honey Squash Purée

4 partridges
3 cups chopped onions
salt and pepper to taste
1 cup celery
1 T. butter
½ cup dry white wine
melted butter for brushing
on partridges

HONEY SQUASH PURÉE:
4 cups cubed peeled butternut squash, 2″ cubes
1½ cups apple juice
2 T. honey
1 tsp. butter
1 tsp. dry tarragon

fresh tarragon sprigs or parsley for garnish

Serves 4

HINT

Partridge is a very delicate bird. After cooking 1 hour, check for doneness quite often.

   Pick and clean partridges. Make sure cavities are clean. Place ¼ cup onions, salt and pepper in each cavity. Place remaining onions, celery and butter in casserole. Top with birds, breast-side-up. Add wine. Cover and bake at 300° for 1½ hours. Remove cover and brush with melted butter. Bake at 350° for 30 minutes to brown. Birds are done when temperature in breasts is 180° or when juices run clear.
   While partridges are cooking, boil squash purée ingredients together until soft. Place in a blender to make purée. Blend until smooth. Put ¾ cup in center of each warm serving plate and set partridges in center. Garnish with fresh tarragon sprigs or fresh parsley.

Small Game Satisfiers

Rabbit/Squirrel with
Green and Black Olives

Rabbit/Squirrel with Green and Black Olives

2 rabbits or squirrels, cut into 6 pieces
2½ cups diced seeded tomatoes
½ cup olive oil
¼ cup all-purpose flour
2 cups chopped onions
1 cup diced red peppers
2½ cups dry white wine
1 cup halved pitted green olives
½ cup halved black olives
2 bay leaves
1 T. dry parsley flakes
1 T. dry thyme
1 T. dry basil
1 tsp. salt
½ tsp. black pepper

HINT

This recipe works very well with all upland game birds and water fowl.

Clean and cut game into pieces. Cut tomatoes into quarters and press out seeds and dice. Heat oil in a heavy oven-proof frying pan. Roll rabbit pieces in flour and place in oil. Brown on all sides. Remove rabbits and set aside.

Add onions and red peppers to pan and sauté until tender. Add flour left from dusting and stir well to combine. Cook on low for 2 minutes, stirring to keep from sticking. Slowly add white wine. Stir until thickened to make a sauce.

Return rabbit pieces to pan with remaining ingredients. Gently stir to combine. Cover and bake at 350° for 2 hours, or until game is tender. Remove bay leaves.

Serve with rice or pasta.

HASENPFEFFER (GERMAN HARE)

2 rabbits, cut into 6 pieces

MARINADE:
3 cups red wine (German is best)
2 T. brown sugar
¼ cup currant jelly
1 T. lemon juice
1 T. cider vinegar
2 tsp. beef base
1 tsp. salt
1 tsp. black pepper
8 juniper berries
4 bay leaves
4 whole cloves

1 cup all-purpose flour
2 T. butter
2 tsp. vegetable oil
2 cups chopped onions
1 cup sliced carrots, ¼" pieces
1 cup sliced celery, ¼" pieces
6 small gingersnap cookies crushed

Serves 4

HINT

If you don't have juniper berries, use 2 oz. (¼ cup) gin. Also, if you wish, you may add 1½ cups sour cream to blended sauce.

Clean and cut rabbit into pieces. Place in a glass dish. Add all marinade ingredients. Cover and place in refrigerator for 3 days, turning meat occasionally. Remove the rabbit from the marinade. Reserve marinade. Pat rabbit dry. Dredge in flour. Shake off excess flour.

In a Dutch oven, heat butter and oil until hot. Add rabbit and brown on all sides. Pour off excess oil. Add marinade liquid and the vegetables. Cover and bake in a 375° oven for 1½ hours, or until rabbit is tender. Transfer rabbit to a covered casserole dish to keep warm.

Remove bay leaves. Place marinade in a blender and blend until smooth. Remove to saucepan. Bring to a boil and add crushed gingersnap cookies. Stir well to combine. Pour over rabbit and serve with spaetzle or noodles.

APPLE RABBIT WITH BLUE PLUM PRUNES

2 rabbits, cut into 6 pieces
¼ cup vegetable oil
¼ cup all-purpose flour
1 cup chopped red onion
1 cup sliced carrots, ¼″ pieces
1 cup cubed, peeled red apples, ½″ cubes
1½ cups whole milk
1 cup sweet white wine
2 tsp. beef base
2 bay leaves
1 tsp. black pepper
1 tsp. salt
½ tsp. dry thyme
2 cups pitted blue plum prunes
¼ cup currant jelly

Clean rabbit. Remove all fat and sinews. Cut rabbit into 6 pieces. Heat oil in a large skillet. Dredge rabbit in flour. Shake off excess flour and sauté rabbit until lightly brown. Remove rabbit. Set aside. Add onions and carrots to skillet, and sauté until tender. Add remaining flour left from dusting. Cook on low heat for 3 minutes, stirring to keep from sticking.

Add apples, milk, wine, beef base, spices and rabbit. Cover and bake for 1 hour in a 350° oven. Remove from oven. Gently stir to keep sauce from sticking to bottom. Add prunes and currant jelly and bake ½ hour larger. Test for doneness. When rabbit is tender, remove bay leaf and serve with mashed potatoes, rice or pasta.

HINT

Of course, squirrel or upland game birds work well. If you want a little tang, use buttermilk instead of whole milk.

FORESTER'S BAKED RABBIT

1 rabbit 3-3½ lbs.
¾ cup seasoned flour (add salt and pepper)
½ cup vegetable oil
2 cups medium cream sauce (see recipe p. 174)
1½ cups heavy cream
1 cup chicken stock (see recipe p. 186)
1 bay leaf
2 medium-sized potatoes
4 carrots, cut into 4″ long pieces
1½ cups sliced onions, ½″ slices
1½ cups quartered fresh mushrooms
3 T. cream sherry
3 T. dry white wine

Serves 4

Clean rabbit and cut in quarters. Dredge in seasoned flour. Heat oil in skillet and brown rabbit. Place rabbit in a large casserole. Add cream sauce, cream chicken stock and bay leaves. Cover tightly and bake for 2 hours at 350˚.

Peel and cut potatoes in half. Peel and cut carrots into 4″ long pieces. Cut onions into ½″ slices. Wash and quarter mushrooms.

Add vegetables, sherry and wine to rabbit and bake until carrots and potatoes are tender. Remove bay leaf and serve.

The recipe takes some work but it is well worth it!

CHARGRILLED PEPPERCORN-CRUSTED RABBIT LOINS AND LEGS

MARINADE:
1½ cups apple juice
3 bay leaves
1 tsp. ground allspice
1 tsp. freshly ground black pepper
4 rabbit loins
4 rabbit rear legs
½ tsp. liquid smoke
½ tsp. ground ginger

1 medium onion, sliced ¼" thick
2 T. peppercorn mix (red, green and black)
1 T. kosher salt
fig peach salsa

HINT

I use a spray olive oil. Make sure your grill is medium hot. Baste with liquid while cooking.

Combine marinade ingredients in a saucepan. Simmer for 5 minutes over medium heat. Remove from heat and chill.

Remove bones from rabbit loin and rear legs. Place meat in a glass dish; cover with cold marinade and onion. Let stand overnight.

Grind peppercorn mix in mill or place in plastic bag and, using a rolling pin, coarsely crush. Add salt. Remove meat from marinade and roll in peppercorn mixture. Spray with oil and chargrill. Serve with fig peach salsa.

This can also be made with squirrel or pheasant.

This recipe works the same for squirrel. It also goes well with spaetzle, noodles, large baked potatoes, or of course, dumplings.

RABBIT QUARTERS WITH WILD MUSHROOMS AND MASHED POTATOES

2 rabbits, cut into quarters (see following recipe)
1 T. butter
½ cup diced shallots or red onion
4 cups quartered fresh mushrooms
½ cup sherry
2 cups rabbit stock
1 cup heavy cream
¼ cup roux (see recipe p. 172)
1 tsp. salt
¼ tsp. white pepper
mashed potatoes

Serves 6

Cook rabbit. Place butter in saucepan. Add shallots and cook until clear. Add mushrooms and sherry and cook for 3 minutes. In a blender, place rabbit stock, cream roux, salt and white pepper. Blend on slow speed until smooth. Add to mushroom base. Add rabbit pieces. Cover and bake for 25 minutes at 375°. Remove from oven. Serve rabbit pieces over mashed potatoes and top with sauce.

TO COOK RABBITS & SQUIRRELS

2 rabbits or squirrels, cut into pieces
1 cup seasoned flour (add salt and pepper)
1 T. salt
1 tsp. black pepper
1 cup vegetable oil
1 qt. chicken stock (see recipe p. 186)
1½ cup chopped onions
1 sachet bag (see recipe p. 186)
¼ cup roux (see recipe p. 172)

Serves 4

HINT

To make a mushroom sauce, add 1 cup sliced fresh mushrooms to roux.

Clean, skin and cut rabbit or squirrel into 6 pieces. Remove all fat, shot and bruised meat.

Place flour, salt and pepper in pie plate and toss to combine. Heat oil to about 375° in an electric fry pan. Dredge game pieces in flour. Place in oil and brown. Remove to Dutch oven. Place chicken stock, onions and sachet bag in Dutch oven. Bake at 375° for 2½-3 hours, checking for doneness after 2 hours. Meat is done when it separates from the bone when pressed with a fork.

To thicken sauce, remove meat to a covered dish. Strain liquid and return to pan. Add ¼ cup roux. Heat to a slow bubble and simmer for 15 minutes, stirring often. Return meat to pan and cook until meat is hot.

Rabbit in the Flowerpot
with Butter Pastry Dough

Rabbit in the Flowerpot

2 cooked rabbits deboned (see how to cook rabbit p. 105)
1 T. butter
1½ cups sliced carrots, ¼″ slices
1½ cups diced onions
2 cups quartered mushrooms
1½ cup frozen green beans
2 cups cubed unpeeled potatoes, ½″ cubes
2 cups rabbit stock
2 10½-oz. cans mushroom soup
1 T. Worcestershire sauce
1 tsp. salt
1 tsp. black pepper
pastry crust for topping (see recipe p. 187)
½ cup egg wash (see recipe p. 188)

Serves 6

Cook rabbit. Cool and remove meat from bones.

In a large soup pot, heat butter and add mushrooms, carrots and onions. Cook until onions are soft. Add potatoes, stock, mushroom soup, Worcestershire sauce, salt and pepper and simmer for 5 minutes, stirring gently to combine. Place stew in Dutch oven or covered casserole with rabbit meat and bake for ½ hour at 350°.

With foil, line 6 new clay flowerpots that have been washed. Brush outsides of pots with vegetable oil. Spoon stew evenly into pots, leaving ½″ on top for crust.

Place round pastry crust pieces on top. Brush with egg wash. Cut small hole in center to let out steam. Bake at 375° for 20 to 25 minutes until crust is browned. For garnish, place two green onions white side down in center hole.

Serve with long spoon and a smile.

HINT

When pressing foil into pot, be gentle, making sure not to tear foil. Trim excess foil so it is even with the rim of the flowerpot.

Campfire Rabbit Stew with
Baking Powder Dumplings

CAMPFIRE RABBIT STEW WITH DUMPLINGS

5 cups water
2 rabbits, cut into 6 pieces
2 cups celery pieces, 1" pieces
¼ cup chicken base
4 cups cubed potatoes, 1"cubes
2 cups cubed onions, 1" cubes
2 cups sliced carrots, ¼" slices
1 tsp. dry thyme
2 cups frozen peas, thawed
2 cups halved mushrooms
½ cup all-purpose flour
½ tsp. freshly ground black pepper
Baking Powder Dumplings (see recipe p. 57)

Serves 8

In a Dutch oven, place water, rabbits, celery and chicken base. Cover and cook over medium heat for 1 hour. Skim off the fat. If you wish, you can remove the meat from the bones. Add potatoes, onions, carrots and thyme. Cover and cook for 45 minutes.

In a bowl, place peas, mushrooms, flour and black pepper. Toss to combine, leaving no flour lumps. Add to stew and gently mix. Cook for 20 minutes.

Make dumplings. Place in stew. Cover and cook for 10 minutes or until dumplings are tender.

You can use chicken stock in place of the water and chicken base, if you wish.

HINT

This is a great camp recipe. If you are using it for camping, you must first prepare at home by precutting the vegetables. Place the vegetables and dry ingredients in bags.

Water Fowl
Delight

Roasted Wild Geese and Ducks

ROASTING WILD GEESE AND DUCKS

1 large or 2 small geese or ducks
Salt Water Soak (see recipe below)
1 T. salt
1 tsp. black pepper
1 onion, cut into 4 pieces
1 lemon, cut in half
1 cup dry white wine
1 large roasting bag

SALT WATER SOAK:
1 gallon cold water
3 T. salt

Clean geese and ducks inside and out. Soak in cold salted water for 1 hour. Remove and drain well. Remove all shot as best as you can.

Season inside of birds with salt and pepper. Place lemon and onion pieces in the cavity. Place birds in a roasting bag. Add wine, seal bag and place in a roasting pan. Bake at 300° until birds are tender to the touch and internal temperature is 180°. The breast should start to separate from the breastbone.

Remove birds from the bag. Cut into desired pieces. Discard lemon, onion and juice.

HINT

For teal and small birds, use smaller amounts of onion and lemon pieces. All fowl must be cooked to an internal temperature of 180° in the thickest part of the breast.

Baked Goose or Duck in Mushroom Wild Rice

BAKED GOOSE OR DUCK IN MUSHROOM WILD RICE

2 ducks, cut into quarters
3 cups chicken stock
(see recipe p. 186)
2 cans cream of celery soup
2 cups halved fresh mushrooms
1½ cups uncooked wild rice

1 cup diced red onion
½ cup sunflower seeds
1 T. Worcestershire Sauce
2 bay leaves
½ tsp. black pepper

Clean and cut birds into quarters. In a large Dutch oven, place all ingredients. Cover and bake at 325° for 3 hours, until rice and meat are tender. Remove bay leaves.

DUCK OR GOOSE AND SAUERKRAUT

2 medium-sized ducks,
or 1 large goose
¼ cup all-purpose flour
¼ cup vegetable oil
1 cup diced onion
1 cup dry white wine

1 cup chicken stock
(see recipe p. 186)
2 T. brown sugar
1 T. chicken base
2 tsp. caraway seed
1 tsp. black pepper, freshly ground
4 cups sauerkraut

Clean and cut ducks into quarters. Remove wings. Trim off all excess fat and skin. Dredge in flour. Shake off excess flour. Heat oil in a Dutch oven. Add duck and brown well on all sides. Add onion and cook until tender. Add remaining flour and stir to combine. Add wine, chicken stock, brown sugar, chicken base and spices. With a wooden spoon, stir brown bits off the bottom of pan.

Rinse sauerkraut under cold water to remove salt. Drain well and add to duck mixture. Combine gently. Cover and bake in a 350° oven for 2 hours. When ducks are tender, serve with Czech dumplings, spaetzle or boiled potatoes. A good German beer tastes great also!

This recipe only gets better the next day.

HINTS

This could also be cooked in a large slow cooker or roasting bag.

You may use 1 large goose. If the goose is large, cut the breast into 4 pieces and separate the leg from the thigh. Two small geese are the same as one large goose.

Goose Breast Fettucini Primavera

6 goose breast pieces
1 T. garlic salt
1 T. freshly ground black pepper
½ cup olive oil
2 cups chopped onions
2 cups red pepper chunks, 1" chunks
½ cup all-purpose flour
3 cups diced tomatoes and liquid
3 cups dry red wine
2 cups beef stock (see recipe p. 186)
2 cups quartered mushrooms
2 cups sliced zucchini, ¼" slices
24 oz. uncooked fettucini or egg noodles
1 cup Parmesan cheese
1 T. chopped fresh basil

Serves 6

Trim off all silver skin from breast and cut breast in pieces the size of your little finger. In a glass bowl, toss the fingers of meat with garlic salt and pepper. Cover and refrigerate 2 hours (no longer).

In a large skillet, heat oil until almost smoke hot. Add goose fingers and brown on all sides. Remove goose fingers to a dish. Set aside.

Add onions and red peppers to skillet. Cook until onions are tender. Add flour and gently combine with vegetables. Add tomato and liquid, red wine, beef stock, mushrooms, zucchini and goose fingers. Simmer 30 minutes over low heat, stirring occasionally to keep from sticking.

Cook fettucini or noodles as directed on package. Drain well. Toss with Parmesan cheese and basil. Place fettucini on a large plate. Top with a generous portion of goose sauce.

Sauce can be made in advance and reheated.

HINT

I also sprinkle a few sliced black olives on top. You can use duck breast and de-boned thighs in this recipe.

ROASTED GOOSE WITH LEMON HERB CRUST

4 goose breasts

MARINADE:
2 T. olive oil
1 T. German mustard
2 cloves garlic, minced fine
1/2 tsp. thyme
1/2 tsp. rosemary
1/2 tsp. black pepper
1 T. lemon juice

CRUST:
1 1/2 cups fresh whole wheat bread crumbs (see recipe p. 172)
2 T. melted butter
1 tsp. marjoram
1/2 tsp. basil
1 tsp. mint leaves
1/2 tsp. lemon zest, grated fine
1/2 tsp. black pepper, freshly ground
1/2 cup flour

HINT

Breast may seem a little rare. If you wish the breast well done, bake to desired doneness.

To marinate breasts: Remove breast from birds. Remove skin and silver skin. Place all marinade ingredients in a glass bowl and whisk well. Add breasts. Cover and refrigerate 2 days.

To make crust: Make fresh wheat bread crumbs. In a bowl, add melted butter and remaining crust ingredients to make crumb crust.

Remove breast from marinade and roll in flour. Shake off excess flour. Then coat with crumb mixture. Press to coat well. Place in a covered casserole dish and bake at 375° for 30 minutes. Gently turn breast and bake 30 minutes uncovered.

Serve with wild rice.

Shovel Duck Stir Fry

SHOVEL DUCK STIR FRY

3 ducks
1/4 cup vegetable oil
3 cups sliced zucchini, 1/4" rounds
2 cups thinly sliced onions
1 cup sliced carrots, 1/4" rounds
1 clove garlic, minced
1 cup sliced fresh mushrooms, 1/4" thick
1 cup sliced green onions
1/2 cup sliced water chestnuts
1/4 cup soy sauce
1 T. lemon juice
2 tsp. diced fresh ginger
1 cup chicken stock (see recipe p. 186)
1/4 cup cornstarch
1/2 tsp. salt
1/2 tsp. freshly ground black pepper

HINT

This is an excellent item to take with you on an outing.

Debone meat from duck. Remove skin, silver skin and sinews. Cut meat into matchstick strips. In a wok or large heavy skillet, heat oil until almost smoke hot. Add duck and quickly stir fry until brown. Skim out duck and set aside.

Return oil to very hot. Add zucchini, onions, carrots and garlic. Sauté until onions are clear. (Do not overcook.) Add duck strips, mushrooms, green onions, water chestnuts, soy sauce, lemon juice and ginger. Sauté for 2 minutes. Combine chicken stock and cornstarch to a smooth liquid. Add to wok. Return to a boil and cook until liquid is clear.

Adjust seasoning with salt and black pepper.

Serve with rice or wild rice.

Wild Duck Tamed with Oranges

4 medium or 2 large wild ducks
1 qt. fresh orange juice
1½ cups diced onions
1 cup diced carrots
½ cup uncooked pearl barley

2 cloves garlic, minced
2 tsp. black pepper
½ tsp. ground nutmeg
¼ tsp. ground cloves
¼ tsp. dry thyme

Serves 4

Cut ducks into 4 pieces and place all ingredients into a slow cooker. Cover and simmer at 250° for 6 hours, or until ducks are tender and meat almost comes off the bone.

Peas, Cabbage, Pears and Duck

2 ducks, cut into 6 pieces
8 strips of bacon, cut into 1″ pieces
1 cup diced onion
½ cup diced celery
2 cloves garlic, minced
½ cup all-purpose flour
1 head green cabbage, cut into 2″ cubes

⅓ cup apple juice
1 tsp. salt
1 tsp. dry tarragon
½ tsp. freshly ground black pepper
2 cups diced fresh pears, 1″ pieces
1½ cups frozen peas, thawed

Clean, skin and cut each duck into 6 pieces. In a Dutch oven, cook the bacon over medium heat. Add duck pieces, onion, celery and garlic. Cook until vegetables are tender.

Add flour and stir with a wooden spoon to combine. Add cabbage, apple juice, salt, tarragon and pepper. Continue baking, covered, for 1½ hours in a 350° oven. Add pears and bake 20 minutes, or until duck is tender. Remove from oven. Gently add the peas and combine well.

Serve in a soup platter with boiled red potatoes or wild rice.

This recipe is the place to use all those pheasant, duck and goose legs that you did not know how to prepare.

This recipe works well with any fowl.

GRENADIERS OF DUCK WITH SHALLOTS AND MARSALA WINE

2 boneless duck breasts
2 cups milk
1 tsp. salt
1 tsp. black pepper
¾ cup seasoned flour (add salt and pepper)
¼ cup clarified butter (see recipe p. 172)
¼ cup diced shallots
8 large mushroom caps
1 cup brown sauce (see recipe p. 173)
½ cup marsala wine
½ cup dry white wine
1 tsp. chopped parsley

Serves 4

Debone, skin and remove fat from duck breasts. Cut into ½″ fingers and soak in milk for 2 hours. Remove from milk and pat dry. Season with salt and pepper. Roll strips in flour and set on a dry plate.

In a heavy sauté pan, heat butter to a fast bubble. Add shallots and duck fingers. Brown fingers on all sides. Add mushroom caps, brown sauce and wines. Reduce heat and simmer for 10 minutes, stirring occasionally. Add chopped parsley.

To serve: Serve 2 mushroom caps with 4 duck fingers
and sauce over rice, wild rice or noodles.

HINT

There are two things to remember when preparing this dish. First, this recipe should be prepared and served immediately. Second, don't cut the strips of duck breast too thick, or they won't cook properly. If you don't have brown sauce or gravy, it is all right to use premade gravy.

Duck with Apples and Green Bananas

DUCK WITH APPLES AND GREEN BANANAS

2 large ducks, or 4 small ducks
1/3 cup vegetable oil
1/4 cup all-purpose flour
1 cup chopped onion
1 cup sliced carrots
1 cup sliced celery
2 bay leaves
1 cup beef stock (see recipe p. 186)
1 tsp. salt
1 T. butter
3 cups sliced cored apple, 1/2" slices
1/2 cup brown sugar
1/4 cup brandy
2 cups sliced bananas (as green as possible), 1/2" thick

Clean ducks. Remove skin. Cut ducks into quarters. In a Dutch oven, heat oil until very hot. Dredge duck pieces in flour and brown on all sides. Add onion, carrots, celery and bay leaves. Cook until tender. Add beef stock and salt. Cover and bake in a 350° oven for 2 hours, or until duck is tender.

While duck is cooking, make sauce as close to serving time as possible. In a sauté pan, heat butter to a fast bubble. Add apple slices and brown sugar. Cook 1 minute. Add brandy. Bring to a boil. Simmer for 3 minutes over low heat. Add banana slices.

When meat is tender, remove duck from pan. Place on platter and cover with sauce.

Even the most skeptical duck eater will love this recipe.

HINT

You may leave out the brandy and add orange juice instead.

DUCK TOMATO BASIL RAGOUT

3 ducks, skinned and cut into
quarters
2 cups diced tomatoes and juice
2 cups sliced fresh mushrooms
1½ cup beef stock
(see recipe p. 186)
1½ cups dry red wine
1 cup diced red onion
1 cup diced carrots
1 cup sliced celery, ¼" slices

1 cup tomato sauce
⅔ cup uncooked pearl barley
½ cup chopped fresh cilantro
1 T. Worcestershire sauce
1 T. dry basil
2 cloves garlic, minced
2 tsp. salt
1 tsp. freshly ground black pepper
parsley and shredded cheese
for garnish

This is the fun part. Place all ingredients in a slow cooker and cook on low heat for about 8 hours.

Remove from slow cooker to a large soup platter and top with parsley and your favorite shredded cheese.

This is very unique and well worth doing.

DUCK WITH THAI MARINADE

4 small ducks
1 lemon, coarsely chopped
½ cup vegetable oil
1 T. brown sugar
3 cloves garlic, minced fine

1 tsp. ground coriander seeds
1 tsp. freshly ground black pepper
½ tsp. dry thyme
½ tsp. ground ginger
¼ tsp. red pepper

Pick ducks and clean cavity well. Combine remaining ingredients. Place duck in large bowl with marinade. Cover and let stand 3 days.

Place duck and 1 cup marinade in roasting bag. Seal bag and place in roasting pan. Bake at 300° for 2½ hours, until duck breast starts to separate from breast bone. Remove and serve with white rice.

HINT

This will spice up even more if you add fresh hot peppers to the marinade. Yes, use "picked" ducks as skinned ducks will dry out when baking.

WINGED TACOS

4 cups cubed goose or duck meat
½ cup taco seasoning
8 taco shells
⅓ cup olive oil

TOPPINGS:
3 cups shredded lettuce
2 cups diced tomatoes ½″ cubes
1½ cups shredded cheddar cheese
1 cup diced dill pickles
1 cup guacamole
1 cup salsa

Serves 8

Skin and debone meat. Remove all fat, sinews and silver skin. Cut meat into thin strips. Toss strips in taco seasoning.

Heat 8 taco shells in oven to crisp them. Heat oil in heavy skillet. Add meat strips and sauté until brown. Remove to paper-towel-lined dish to absorb oil. Assemble tacos with your favorite toppings and eat.

You should use any fun toppings you like!
I sometimes use diced jalapeño peppers and sour cream.

Peppercorn Pan-Broiled Breast

PEPPERCORN PAN-BROILED BREAST

4 duck breasts
3 T. green peppercorns
1 T. black peppercorns
½ tsp. coarse salt
1 T. olive oil
2 T. balsamic vinegar
2 T. brandy
¼ cup beef stock (see recipe p. 186)
1 tsp. chopped parsley

HINT

You can also use goose breast in this recipe.

Debone the duck. Remove skin, silver skin and sinews. Place breast on a cutting board. In between 2 plastic bags flatten meat to ½″ cutlets with a broad meat mallet. Discard bags and set meat aside. Place green and black peppercorns in plastic bag and gently crack with a mallet. Combine peppercorns and salt and press into cutlets on both sides.

In a heavy skillet, heat oil until almost smoke hot. Add cutlets and brown for 1 minute. Turn and brown 1½ minutes on other side. Remove to a covered dish to keep hot until ready to serve.

Splash skillet with vinegar and brandy. Bring to a vigorous boil. Add beef stock. Cook 4 minutes and serve as sauce with cooked duck breasts. Top with chopped parsley.

I serve boiled potatoes and a green vegetable with this recipe.

Big Game Favorites

Venison Scaloppini
Side dish: Red Cabbage

VENISON SCALOPPINI

8 slices venison roast (3 oz. each)
½ cup seasoned flour (add salt and pepper)
2 tsp. minced fresh parsley
1 tsp. lemon zest
½ tsp. freshly ground black pepper
1 T. clarified butter (see recipe p. 172)
2 T. diced shallots
1 clove garlic, minced
½ cup dry white wine
2 tsp. minced fresh tarragon

HINT

The best cut of meat to use is the tenderloin. Elk and antelope are also delicious this way.

From a boneless roast, remove fat and silver skin. Slice roast into ½″ thick slices across the grain. Flatten slices to ¼″ thick in a plastic bag, using a broad meat mallet. Roll venison in flour. Shake off excess flour. Set aside.

Combine parsley, lemon zest and freshly ground black pepper in a bowl. In a large sauté pan, melt butter. Add shallots and garlic. Top with venison slices. Sauté over medium heat until brown on bottom. Turn venison slices and stir shallots. Sauté until bottoms of slices are brown. Add wine and tarragon. Let simmer for 2 minutes.

Remove meat to a heated serving platter. Sprinkle parsley mixture over venison. Top with sauce from pan, and serve with pasta, egg noodles or spaetzle.

Venison Currant Mole

VENISON CURRANT MOLE

1 lb. venison loin or round, cut ½″ slices
1 cup seasoned flour (add salt and pepper)
¼ cup clarified butter (see recipe p. 172)
½ cup diced shallots

2 cups brown sauce (see recipe p. 173)
½ cup cream sherry
⅓ cup red currant jam or jelly
1 T. shaved dark chocolate

HINT

This works with all game meat.

Serves 4

Remove fat and silver skin from venison. Slice venison into twelve ½″ slices. Flatten to ¼″ with mallet. Dredge slices in flour. Heat butter to a fast bubble in a heavy sauté pan. Add shallots and venison. Sauté until venison slices are brown. Turn and sauté for 30 seconds, being careful not to brown shallots.

Add brown sauce, currant jelly, sherry and chocolate shavings. Simmer 10 minutes on low heat, stirring gently from time to time to prevent sticking.

GAME SAUTÉ WITH CARAMELIZED ONIONS AND PLUM CONFITURE

*CARAMELIZED ONIONS
AND PLUMS:*
¼ cup butter
3 cups thinly sliced onions,
cut into quarters
6 blue plums, pitted and cut in half
½ cup beef stock (see recipe p. 186)
1 T. brown sugar
⅓ cup sherry

1 tsp. dry sage leaves
½ tsp. black pepper

MEAT:
8 slices lean game (2 oz. each)
1 cup seasoned flour (add salt and pepper)
2 tsp. poultry seasoning
2 T. clarified butter (see recipe p. 172)

In a saucepan, heat butter. Add onions and cook for 10 minutes on low heat. Add plum halves, stock, sherry, brown sugar, sage and pepper. Simmer on low heat for 15 minutes, until all liquid is evaporated. Sauce should look like jam. Set aside.

Remove fat and silver skin from meat and slice into cutlets. Pound cutlets flat. Combine flour and poultry seasoning. Dredge slices in flour. Shake off excess flour.

In a heavy skillet, heat butter to a fast bubble. Add meat and brown on both sides. Add sauce and simmer over low heat for 2-3 minutes.

Serve game slices with a generous amount of sauce.

Game Schnitzel

GAME SCHNITZEL

1 lb. game roast, cut into ½″ slices
1 cup seasoned flour (add salt and pepper)
1 cup egg wash (see recipe p. 188)
3 cups fresh white bread crumbs (see recipe p. 172)
¼ cup clarified butter (see recipe p. 172)
2 T. fresh lemon juice
12 lemon slices to garnish

Serves 4

Remove all fat, sinews and silver skin from meat. Cut game meat into twelve ½″ thick slices. Flatten to ¼″ thickness in a plastic bag using a meat mallet. Do not overpound and tear the meat.

Dredge game slices in seasoned flour. Dip in egg wash and then in bread crumbs. Shake off excess crumbs. Heat clarified butter in a large sauté pan. When butter starts to bubble, add game slices and brown. Turn slices over and splash with lemon juice. Cover and bake in a 350° oven for about 15 minutes. Place three schnitzels on each plate and garnish each schnitzel with a lemon slice.

VARIATIONS:

SCHNITZEL HOLSTEIN: Place 2 eggs fried sunny-side up, 2 strips of anchovies and 12 capers on top of each portion of schnitzels before serving.

SCHNITZEL HUNTER'S-STYLE: Cook schnitzels per recipe above and cover with mushroom sauce. (See recipe on page 174).

SCHNITZEL ITALIAN-STYLE: Finish cutlets by topping with tomato sauce and provolone cheese. Melt cheese under broiler and serve.

CAPER SCHNITZEL: Serve with ¼ cup of caper sauce (see recipe on page 176) over each portion.

HINT

Schnitzels should be free from all fat and connective tissue. They should be sliced thin and shaped into an oval or triangle. For game schnitzels, garnish with hot, fresh orange cranberry sauce. Don't take a shortcut on the bread crumbs. Make them fresh. You will taste the difference.

Gorgonzola-Filled Venison Roll

GORGONZOLA-FILLED VENISON ROLL

MEAT MIXTURE:
1 lb. ground venison meat
½ lb. ground pork
2 eggs, beaten
½ cup fresh bread crumbs (see recipe p. 172)
1 tsp. salt
1 tsp. black pepper

FILLING MIXTURE:
⅔ cup grated carrots
½ cup crumbled Gorgonzola cheese
½ cup fresh bread crumbs (see recipe p. 172)
½ tsp. garlic powder

Combine all meat mixture ingredients and mix well. On a flat surface, place a double-thick sheet (1½ feet long) of foil (the wider the better). Place meat on the foil and flatten to 1″ thickness.

In a large bowl, gently combine all filling ingredients. Place the filling mixture 3″ from the bottom edge of the flattened meat and roll meat into a cylinder, enclosing in foil. Crimp the ends of the foil and bake at 350° for 1 hour. Remove from the foil. Slice and serve.

Blue cheese works very well instead of Gorgonzola. Of course, you can use all kinds of red game meats.

Roast Rack of Venison Hunter's Style

ROAST RACK OF VENISON HUNTER'S STYLE

3- to 3½-lb. rack of venison
olive oil spray
8 shallots, peeled and cut in half
12 mushrooms, cut in half
1 cup dry red wine
6 strips bacon
1 cup brown sauce or gravy (see recipe p. 173)
3 T. gin
1 tsp. dry thyme
1 tsp. black pepper, freshly ground
½ tsp. salt

Remove all fat and silver skin from meat and rib bones. Spray a roasting pan with olive oil spray. Place shallots and mushrooms in bottom of a roasting pan. Add red wine.

Place bacon strips over meat evenly to cover. Secure with toothpicks. Preheat oven to 450°. Set rack, bone side down, in pan on top of vegetables. Place in oven and let brown for 2 minutes. Reduce heat to 250° and roast about 35-45 minutes to an internal temperature of 130° for medium rare. Transfer to a plate and cover with foil. Add brown sauce, gin, thyme, pepper and salt to vegetables. Mix gently. Bring to a boil. Skim off the fat.

To serve roast, remove toothpicks. Cut into slices 1½"-2" thick, depending on the width of the rib bones. Serve 2 slices topped with mushroom sauce.

The reason we put bacon on top of the meat is to add flavor and keep it moist.
If you wish, you can remove bacon before serving. I like it left on.

HINT

This is a preparation you need to have in mind before you take your harvested venison to be cut up. I have the butcher cut this out of the center of the bone-in loins. This only works well with smaller-sized game racks. Elk and moose are too large.

Rum Runner Roast

RUM RUNNER ROAST

2½ to 3 lb. game roast
¼ cup vegetable oil
2 cups chopped onions, 1" pieces
1½ cups chopped carrots, 1" pieces
1½ cups chopped yellow turnips,
1" pieces
3 cups beef stock (see recipe p. 186)
1 cup chili sauce
⅔ cup dark raisins

½ cup dark rum
⅓ cup molasses
1 T. beef base
2 tsp. dry thyme
1 tsp. black pepper
½ cup dry red wine
1 T. Worcestershire sauce
2 tsp. cornstarch

Trim off all fat and silver skin from roast. In a Dutch oven, heat oil until smoke hot. Add roast and brown on all sides. Remove roast. Add vegetables and cook for 4 minutes to lightly brown. Pour off excess oil. Return roast to Dutch oven.

Add beef stock, chili sauce, raisins, rum, molasses, beef base, thyme and black pepper. Bake in a 350° oven for 2 hours. Combine red wine, Worcestershire sauce and cornstarch to make a smooth paste. Add to liquid and stir to combine. Return to oven for 20 minutes. Remove roast and slice into thick pieces. Serve with vegetable sauce.

BAVARIAN CHOPS

4 loin chops, 1" thick
½ cup seasoned flour (add salt
and pepper)
¼ cup butter
2 cups sliced mushrooms
½ cup sliced green onions

½ cup dry white wine
1 T. drained capers
2 tsp. lemon juice
1 tsp. dry thyme
1 10½-oz. can cream of
celery soup

Remove fat and silver skin from outside of chops. Dust chops in flour. In a large skillet, heat butter to a fast bubble. Add chops and brown on both sides. Add mushrooms, green onions, wine, capers, lemon juice and thyme and simmer for 5 minutes on medium heat. Add celery soup. Stir to combine. Cover and cook for 30 minutes.

Serve over spaetzle or egg noodles.

Easy Lemon Pepper Chops

8 loin chops, 1" thick
2 tsp. dry thyme
1½ tsp. freshly ground pepper
2 tsp. lemon zest
1 tsp. garlic salt
1 T. olive oil
2 tsp. Worcestershire sauce

Trim off all fat and silver skin from meat. Combine thyme, lemon zest, pepper, and garlic salt. Rub on both sides of chops. Let stand for 10 minutes.

In a heavy skillet, heat olive oil. Add chops and brown well on both sides. Cook to medium rare. Splash with Worcestershire sauce. Turn chops and serve.

This recipe also works well with upland game bird breast.

Steak and Chop Rub

2 T. lemon pepper
2 T. coarsely ground black pepper
2 T. onion powder
1 T. garlic powder
1 T. kosher or coarse salt
1 T. Hungarian paprika
2 tsp. dry mustard
2 tsp. ground ginger
1 tsp. ground allspice
olive oil

Place all ingredients, except olive oil, in a bowl and blend well. Rub on steak or chops 30 minutes before grilling. Place chops in a plastic bag with a small amount of olive oil. This softens the spices so as not to cause a burnt crust.

HINT

Do not put rub spices on too thick or you'll get a burnt crust. If you wish to leave out the salt, rub meat and keep in plastic bag overnight. Just before grilling, sprinkle with salt to draw out the moisture if used overnight.

KABOBS

16 cubes of game meat, 1" cubes
2 cups herb salad dressing
8 jumbo fresh mushrooms
1 cup sherry
8 pearl onions or shallots
8 cubes of red or green peppers, 2" cubes
8 cubes of fresh pineapple
8 slices zucchini, 1/2" thick
4 12" bamboo or metal skewers

Serves 4

Remove fat and silver skin from game meat and cut meat into 1″cubes. Place in a glass or stainless steel bowl. Cover with herb dressing and refrigerate for approximately 72 hours.

Cut stems from mushrooms and simmer in sherry until tender. Drain liquid and reserve. Set mushrooms aside. Peel and blanch onions in 1 quart salted water until tender. Drain off the liquid and set onions aside. Bring 1 quart salted water to boil. Add peppers. When water returns to a boil, remove the peppers and set aside. Remove skin from pineapple and cut into large cubes making sure not to use the core. Slice zucchini.

Place ingredients on skewers in the following order: mushroom, onion, meat, red or green pepper, zucchini, meat, pineapple, meat, zucchini, red or green pepper, meat, onion and mushroom.

Grill over medium heat until meat and vegetables are done to your liking. While grilling, combine 1 cup meat marinade and liquid from the mushrooms and use to baste the kabobs.

HINT

Use any game or red meat. Use any vegetables you like but precook them first.

Chef John's Game Sauerbraten

Chef John's Game Sauerbraten

MARINADE:
2 cups cold beef stock (see recipe p. 186)
1½ cups red wine vinegar
1½ cups burgundy wine
1 cup thinly sliced onion
½ cup thinly sliced carrots
½ cup thinly sliced celery
2 T. brown sugar
1 T. beef base
1 T. juniper berries
2 cloves garlic, chopped
1 tsp. salt
2 bay leaves
6 crushed black peppercorns
4 whole cloves

GAME MEAT:
4 lbs. game roast (game of choice)
⅓ cup vegetable oil
1 cup crushed gingersnap cookies
⅔ cup raisins

Serves 4-6

HINT

Boneless roast works best.

Put all marinade ingredients into a large container and stir well.

Remove all fat and silver skin from game meat. Pierce meat randomly with boning knife. Add meat to marinade, making sure meat is completely covered with liquid. Refrigerate, covered, for 72 hours. (If you marinate for less than 72 hours, meat will be tough. If you marinate much more than 72 hours, the meat will become dry and flavorless.)

Remove meat, wipe dry with towel and brown in hot oil in a frying pan or skillet. Remove to a large pot. Place marinade in with the meat. Cover, bring to a boil, and simmer for 2½ hours, or until meat is tender. When meat is done, transfer to dry pan. Cover with a damp cloth and keep warm.

Remove bay leaves. Purée liquid and vegetables in a blender. Place in a heavy pot, whisk crushed gingersnap cookies into the liquid, stirring until smooth. Add raisins. Simmer for 5 minutes. Hold for service. Cut meat across the grain and serve with a 2 oz. ladle of sauce per portion.

Game Tenderloins with Peppercorn and Cognac Sauce
Side dish: Skillet Camp Potatoes

GAME TENDERLOINS WITH PEPPERCORN AND COGNAC SAUCE

2 venison tenderloins
2 T. peppercorn mix, crushed
2 T. olive oil

SAUCE BASE:
3 cups beef stock (see recipe p. 186)
½ cup diced carrots
½ cup diced onion
1 T. tomato purée
2 cloves garlic, quartered
2 bay leaves
1 tsp. beef base
1 tsp. dry thyme

½ cup V. S. cognac
green onions and horseradish for garnish

Serves 2

(see recipe p. 186)

HINT

For tenderloins from large animals, cut tenders in half the long way. Make sure to remove all side meat, fat and silver skin.

Remove all fat and silver skin from tenderloins. Place peppercorns into a plastic bag and smash with a mallet to a medium texture. Add tenderloins to bag and press in peppercorns firmly. Remove to new bag. Add olive oil and let stand overnight.

Place all sauce ingredients in a heavy saucepan and simmer over low heat to reduce liquid by half. Strain out vegetables and bay leaves. Place liquid in clean saucepan. Add cognac and reduce liquid to half over medium heat. Keep warm.

Heat a skillet until hot. Add oil and tenderloins from bag. Brown on all sides. Place skillet in a 375° oven for about 15 minutes. Remove tenderloins to hot dinner plates. Top with ½ cup hot sauce and garnish with green onions and horseradish.

GRILLED GAME JAMAICAN STYLE

8 steaks (6 oz. each), 1″ thick

SAUCE:
1½ cups diced onions
1 cup olive oil
zest and juice of 1 orange
zest and juice of 1 lemon
2 jalapeño peppers with seeds

2 T. minced fresh ginger
1 tsp. ground nutmeg
1 tsp. ground allspice
1 tsp. ground cinnamon
1 tsp. black pepper
¼ tsp. dry thyme
¼ cup grated fresh ginger for garnish

Trim off fat and silver skin from steaks. Place sauce ingredients in a blender. Blend for 1 minute on high. Place steaks and sauce in covered glass dish and let stand overnight. Grill over medium heat until medium rare. Garnish with grated ginger.

True Jamaicans love their peppers hot.
They use Scotch bonnet or serrano chili peppers.

GAME CHOPS IN GREEN CHILI BEANS

4 bone-in game chops, 1″ thick
1 T. olive oil
1 cup diced onion
2 cups canned butter beans, drained
2 cups diced tomatoes with juice
1 cup diced green chilies, drained
¼ cup chopped fresh cilantro
1½ tsp. red pepper flakes
1 tsp. ground cumin

Remove fat and silver skin from chops. With a sharp knife, cut along bone in center of chop. Leave each end attached.

In a large heavy skillet, heat oil. Add chops. Brown well and turn. Cook to desired doneness. Remove to plate and cover to keep warm. Add onion and cook until tender. With a wooden spoon, scrape all brown pieces from bottom of skillet. Add remaining ingredients and simmer uncovered for 10 minutes. Serve with chops.

HINT

I like this recipe with antelope or caribou steaks. If you like yours milder, leave out the red pepper flakes.

GAME PAPRIKOSH

2 lbs. game meat, cut into 1" cubes
¼ cup vegetable oil
¼ cup all-purpose flour
2 T. Hungarian paprika
3 cups diced onions
2 cups diced tomatoes with juice
2 cups tomato purée
2 tsp. beef base
2 cloves minced garlic
1 tsp. salt
½ tsp. black pepper
2 cups sliced fresh mushrooms
⅔ cup dry red wine
sour cream and parsley flakes for garnish

Serves 4-6

Cube game meat, removing excess fat and connective tissue. Heat oil until almost smoke hot in a heavy sauté pan. Add game meat and brown on all sides. Remove meat and excess oil to a heavy roasting pan or casserole dish.

Combine flour and paprika. Add to meat and mix well with a wooden spoon. Add onions, diced tomatoes, tomato purée, beef base, garlic, salt and pepper. Mix well. Cover and bake for 1 hour at 350°. Add mushrooms and wine. Cover and bake an additional 20 minutes (cubes should be tender to the fork when done). Garnish with a large dollop of sour cream and parsley flakes.

HINT

Red cabbage and Czech dumplings make wonderful accompaniments to this recipe.

HINTS

You may substitute red onions for white onions. I also sometimes use half sherry and half white wine. It make the onions a little sweeter. Any kind of fresh herb works, so use your favorite instead of parsley.

It is all right to use canned brown sauce or gravy. This recipe also works well with duck or goose breasts.

GAME SAUTÉ

8 slices game meat, ¼″ thick
1 T. butter
6 cups sliced white onions
1 cup dry white wine

1 cup seasoned flour (add salt and pepper)
1 T. vegetable oil
1 T. Worcestershire sauce
2 T. dry parsley flakes

Serves 4

Remove fat and silver skin from game. Slice meat ¼″ thick. Flatten with meat mallet. In a heavy skillet, heat butter to a fast bubble. Add onions and sauté over medium heat for 2 minutes. (Do not brown.) Add white wine. Cover and simmer for 5 minutes.

While onions are cooking, dredge game slices in flour and shake off excess flour. In a separate skillet heat oil. Add game and sauté for 1 minute. Turn and sauté 2 minutes. Splash with Worcestershire sauce. Remove from pan. Place game slices on warm plates. Toss onions with parsley and place a generous amount of onions and liquid on venison slices.

CLASSIC VENISON STROGANOFF

12 slices game meat (2 oz. each)
1 cup seasoned flour (add salt and pepper)
½ tsp. salt
¼ tsp. white pepper
¼ cup clarified butter (see recipe p. 172)

½ cup minced shallots
8 fresh mushrooms, cut into quarters
⅔ cup sherry
2 cups brown sauce (see recipe p. 173)
1 cup sour cream

Remove all fat and silver skin from game. Slice meat into 2-ounce slices. Flatten with a meat mallet. Place flour, salt, and white pepper in a pie plate and mix well. Dredge game slices in flour to coat. Shake off excess flour. Set aside.

Place butter in a large frying pan and bring to a fast bubble. Add game slices and cook for 1 minute. Turn and cook other side for 1 minute. Add shallots and mushrooms and cook 1 minute. Add sherry wine, brown sauce and sour cream. Simmer on low heat for 10 minutes. Serve with rice, wild rice or egg noodles.

GAME WITH APPLES, CALVADOS AND CIDER

8 slices red game meat (3 oz. each)
4 green apples, peeled and cut into 1/3" slices
4 T. butter
2/3 cups thinly sliced red onion, cut into quarters
1 T. brown sugar
1/4 cup Calvados or apple brandy
1 T. apple cider
2 tsp. lemon juice
1 tsp. salt
1/2 tsp. dry thyme
1 10 1/2-oz. can mushroom soup
1/2 cup seasoned flour (add salt and pepper)
1 1/2 cups sliced fresh mushrooms

Serves 4

Remove fat and silver skin from meat and flatten meat with a meat mallet to 1/4" thickness. Do not overpound or tear pieces.

Peel, core and slice apples into 1/3" slices. In skillet, heat 2 tablespoons butter to a fast bubble. Add onion and cook until tender. Add apples and brown sugar. Cook 1 minute. Add calvados, apple cider, lemon juice, salt and thyme. Simmer over medium heat to reduce liquid by one half. Add soup and gently combine. Simmer 2 minutes.

While sauce is cooking, heat remaining 2 tablespoons butter in a skillet to a fast bubble. Dredge game slices in seasoned flour. Shake off excess flour and brown on both sides. Add mushrooms and cook until tender.

Place on warm serving platter. Cover with apple mixture. Serve with spaetzle or noodles.

HINT

Do not overcook meat. It is all right to use red apples. If you can't find Calvados or apple brandy, regular brandy will work fine. This is an outstanding way to serve wild boar loins or chops.

Pan Grilled Game with Garden Tomatoes and Basil

4 6-oz. game steaks
2 T. Spanish paprika
2 tsp. freshly ground black pepper
3 cups diced tomatoes
1 T. olive oil
1/4 cup minced shallots

2 cloves garlic, minced
1 cup sliced green onions
1 cup diced red peppers
1/3 cup diced black olives
3 T. minced fresh basil

Remove all fat and silver skin from steaks. Flatten steaks to about 1/2" with a meat mallet. Rub steaks with paprika and black pepper. Place in a plastic bag for 1 hour.

Place diced tomatoes in strainer and let liquid drain.

In a heavy skillet, heat oil. Add steaks and brown well on both sides. Add shallots and garlic and cook 1 minute. Add green tomatoes, onions, red peppers, black olives and basil, and simmer for 3 minutes.

Serve with rice or pasta. Use in other dishes with tomato sauce.

Game Ribeye Parmesan

4 game ribeye steaks, 1" thick
1 1/2 cups fresh bread crumbs
    (see recipe p. 172)
1 cup grated Parmesan cheese
1 tsp. dry basil leaves
1 tsp. dry oregano leaves
1 tsp. onion salt

1/2 tsp. black pepper
1/2 cup all-purpose flour
1 cup egg wash (see recipe p. 188)
2 T. olive oil
2/3 cup diced shallots
red pepper rings and
horseradish to garnish

Serves 4

Trim excess fat and silver skin from steaks. Combine bread crumbs, Parmesan cheese and seasonings in a bowl. Place flour in a pie plate. Place egg wash in a shallow bowl. In a large skillet, heat olive oil. Add shallots and cook until tender.

Dredge steaks in flour. Shake off excess flour. Dip in egg wash and coat with Parmesan cheese mixture. Place steaks in oven-proof skillet and brown. Turn and brown. Bake in a 375° oven for 15 minutes. Serve each steak with a raw red pepper ring filled with horseradish.

Hints

This works well with any fowl or boneless breast meat. Keep the liquid from the tomatoes. It has great flavor for use in other dishes with tomato sauce.

This is very good with all fowl breasts or, of course, with any other game ribeyes.

GAME BURGUNDY WITH FRESH MUSHROOMS

2 lbs. game roast, cut into ½″ cubes
1 cup seasoned flour (add salt and pepper)
8 oz. bacon, diced
3 cloves garlic, minced
¼ cup tomato paste
2 cups cubed onions, ½″ cubes
1½ cups diced carrots
1 cup beef stock (see recipe p. 186)
1 T. brown sugar
2 tsp. beef base
4 cups burgundy wine
1 tsp. thyme
½ tsp. black pepper
2 cups thickly sliced fresh mushrooms

Remove all fat and silver skin from meat. Cut meat into cubes. Roll cubes in flour.

In a Dutch oven over medium heat, cook bacon pieces until light brown. Add game cubes and garlic and cook until game is brown on all sides. Stir with a wooden spoon to keep meat from sticking to bottom. Add remaining flour and combine well. Add wine, onions, carrots, beef stock, tomato paste, brown sugar, beef base, thyme and black pepper. Cover and bake for 1½ hours in a 350° oven. Add mushrooms and bake for 30 minutes longer.

HINT

This works well with all red game meat. Be sure to use a medium to good quality burgundy wine.

Sweet Spicy Antelope Loin Chops

SWEET SPICY ANTELOPE LOIN CHOPS

8 center cut chops, 3/4" -1" thick
1 T. olive oil
4 cloves garlic, peeled
2 green jalapeño peppers, seeds and stems removed

MARINADE:
1/4 cup Worcestershire sauce
1/4 cup Dijon mustard
1/4 cup honey
1 tsp. ground allspice
2 tsp. lemon zest
1/2 tsp. freshly ground black pepper
5 drops hot sauce
1 cup apple juice
1 T. cornstarch

Place a double-thick sheet of foil in a soup bowl. Press to make a pocket. Add oil, garlic and jalapeño peppers. Close foil tightly and place on pie plate. Bake for 1 hour at 350°. Remove from oven and let cool.

Place jalapeño pepper mixture and marinade ingredients in blender and purée until smooth.

Remove all fat and silver skin from chops. Place in a glass casserole dish. Add marinade. Cover and let stand overnight.

Remove chops and grill over medium heat until medium rare or medium. (Do not overcook!)

Place marinade liquid in a small saucepan. Simmer for 5 minutes over medium heat. Combine apple juice with cornstarch and make a smooth paste. Add to marinade stirring slowly until sauce is clear.

Place 1/4 cup sauce on warm dinner plate. Top with chop and serve with plenty of white rice.

Coconut Antelope Curry

Coconut Antelope Curry

1 lb. antelope, cut into 1″ squares
½ cup seasoned flour (add salt and pepper)
2 T. olive oil
1 cup sliced onion
2 cloves garlic, minced
1 10½-oz. can mushroom soup
1 cup coconut milk
1 cup beef stock (see recipe p. 186)
1 T. beef base
1 T. curry powder
2 small jalapeño peppers, minced with seeds
1 tsp. dry mustard
1 tsp. freshly ground black pepper
½ cup cashew pieces
½ cup shredded coconut
1 T. honey

Serves 4

HINT

By all means, serve this dish with your favorite chutney. This is an excellent way to prepare game that has a strong wild taste.

Trim all fat, silver skin and sinews from meat. Cut meat into cubes. Dredge in flour. Shake off excess flour. In a Dutch oven, heat oil until almost smoke hot. Add antelope cubes. Brown well on all sides. Remove meat to a plate. Add onions and garlic and cook until tender. Add mushroom soup, coconut milk, beef stock, beef base, curry powder, jalapeño peppers, dry mustard, black pepper. Combine well. Add cooked meat. Cover and bake in a 350° oven for 2 hours.

Place nuts and coconut in a bowl. Toss with honey to coat well. Place on a well-buttered sheet pan. Spread out evenly into a thin layer. Place in 350° oven and bake for 20 minutes, or until golden brown. Remove from oven. Let cool on pan. Serve antelope curry over white rice topped with honey-coconut-cashew pieces.

I line my sheet pan with foil, as it is much easier to clean. If you can't find coconut milk, use piña colada mix.

HINT

It is best to use meat from the round. The slice should be 3"-4" wide and 6"-8" long after pounding.

CLASSIC GAME ROLL-UP

GAME MEAT:
12 slices of game meat (4-6 oz. each)
salt and pepper to taste
½ cup spicy German mustard
3 cups uncooked bread stuffing
12 pickle spears
6 frankfurters, cut in half lengthwise
36 onion strips, ¼" thick
1 cup vegetable oil
1 cup seasoned flour (add salt and pepper)

SAUCE:
2 10½-oz. cans mushroom soup
1½ cups diced onions
1 cup diced mushrooms
1 cup dry red wine
1 cup beef stock (see recipe p. 186)
¾ cup tomato purée
½ cup chili sauce
1 T. beef base
½ tsp. ground black pepper

Serves 6

Pound game slices flat with a mallet. Season with salt and pepper. Spread 1 teaspoon mustard over each slice.

Put ¼ cup stuffing in center of each slice. On stuffing, place pickle, frankfurter piece and 3 onion strips. Roll up. Put toothpicks through roll-ups to hold together.

Heat oil in a heavy skillet. Dredge roll-ups in seasoned flour. Shake off excess flour. Brown in hot oil. Remove from pan and place in casserole.

Place all sauce ingredients in a bowl and mix well. Pour over roll-ups. Cover and bake at 350°, until meat is tender to a fork (about 1½ hours).

Remove toothpicks and serve two roll-ups per person with ½ cup sauce. Serve with wild rice, noodles or spaetzles. There is a lot of sauce.

BARBECUE GAME PIES

1 lb. game roast cut into ½" cubes
1 T. Hungarian paprika
1 tsp. black pepper
½ cup olive oil
1 cup diced onions
1 cup diced carrots
1 cup peeled and diced celery
1 cup diced turnips
3 cloves garlic, minced
1 cup biscuit mix
1 cup beef stock (see recipe p. 186)
1 cup barbecue sauce
2 tsp. Worcestershire sauce
1 tsp. beef base
1 cup diced potatoes
1 cup coarsely chopped fresh mushrooms
pie crust for 2 double-crusted pies (see recipe p. 188)

Makes 2 pies

Trim fat and silver skin from game. Cut game into cubes. Toss cubes with paprika and black pepper, and place in plastic bag for one hour. Heat ¼ cup olive oil in a large skillet. Add meat and brown. Remove meat to dish leaving oil in skillet.

Add remaining oil to skillet and heat. Add onions, carrots, celery, turnips and garlic and cook until tender. Add biscuit mix. Gently stir to combine and to keep from sticking. Cook over low heat for 2 minutes.

Add beef stock, barbecue sauce, Worcestershire sauce and beef base. Stir to make a sauce. Remove to a Dutch oven and add venison, potatoes and mushrooms. Cover and bake in a 350° oven for 1 hour.

Make pie crust. Place crust in bottom of two pie pans. Add venison filling and top each pie with crust. Seal and bake at 350° for 45-55 minutes, or until crust is golden brown. Cut into fourths and serve.

HINT

For individual servings, put game filling in ovenproof bowls topped with puff pastry circles and bake at 375° for 20 minutes.

Moose Steaks with Green Chili Pockets

MOOSE STEAKS WITH GREEN CHILI POCKETS

4 moose steaks (8-10 oz. each)

RUB:
1 T. black pepper
1 T. Cajun seasoning
½ tsp. garlic powder
2 tsp. olive oil

STUFFING:
2 T. olive oil
1 cup diced onion
1 cup canned green chilies
1 tsp. dry oregano
1 tsp. dry basil
¾ cup bread crumbs (see recipe p. 172)

Remove all excess fat and silver skin from steaks. Cut a deep horizontal pocket in each steak. Leave ½″ on the sides and end. Combine black pepper, Cajun seasoning and garlic powder. Rub on steaks and place steaks in plastic bag with 2 teaspoons olive oil overnight.

Heat 2 teaspoons olive oil in skillet. Add onion and sauté until tender. Add green chilies and spices and simmer for 5 minutes over low heat. Add bread crumbs and combine well to make thick paste.

Stuff each steak with 2 tablespoons chili stuffing. Spray outside of steak with olive oil sparay and grill to medium rare.

HINT

If you like it hot, add hot peppers of your choice to stuffing.

GAME MUSHROOM MONSTER POTATOES

6 8-oz. baking potatoes
1½ lbs. boneless game meat
flour
¼ cup butter
1 cup red onion, diced ¼"
2 cloves garlic, minced fine
2 cups fresh mushrooms, sliced ¼"
2 cups wild mushrooms (shiitake or portabello), cut in ½" pieces
2 T. sherry wine
½ tsp. dry mustard
2 tsp. salt
1 tsp. black pepper
2 cups shredded Swiss cheese
1 cup sour cream
1 T. chives, chopped for garnish

Wash and bake potatoes at 375° for about 55 minutes or until they are tender when squeezed. It is better to underbake than overbake. While baking, remove fat and silver skin from meat. Cut in strips the size of your little finger. Dredge in flour and shake off excess.

In a heavy skillet, heat butter. Add game fingers and brown on all sides. Add onions, garlic, mushrooms and cook 2 minutes on medium heat, tossing meat to keep from sticking. Add sherry wine and simmer for 5 minutes.

Dissolve dry mustard in 2 T. hot broth from mushrooms and sherry liquid. Add to sauce with salt and pepper.

To serve: Place potato in center of warm dinner plate. Split potato in center, pressing apart to make a canoe. Place the mushroom mixture evenly inside potato. Top with generous amount of cheese and a dollop of sour cream and garnish with chopped chives.

DUTCH OVEN BAKED GAME

2 lbs. boneless red game meat, cut into 2″ cubes
¼ cup olive oil
½ cup flour
2 cloves garlic, minced fine
2 cups onions, cubed 1″
1½ cups parsnips or carrots, cut in ¼″ slices
½ tsp. nutmeg
1 tsp. black pepper
1 T. beef base
2 cups beef stock (see recipe p. 186)
1 cup dry sherry
2 cups fresh mushrooms, cut in ¼″ slices
1 cup light sour cream
2 T. tomato paste

Serves 4

Remove bones, fat and silver skin from game and cut into 2″ cubes. Heat oil to almost smoke hot. Roll cubes in flour and shake off excess flour thoroughly. Add to oil and brown on all sides. Remove to a Dutch oven.

To the skillet add garlic, onions, parsnips/carrots and cook until tender. Add flour and gently combine. Add to meat. Add nutmeg, pepper, beef base, beef stock and sherry. Combine well. Cover and bake in a 350° oven for 1½ hours. Add mushrooms, sour cream, tomato paste and bake for 30 minutes.

This dish goes well with literally everything. It also tastes even better the next day.

HINT

I finish this with baking powder dumplings. If using dumplings, add 1 extra cup of beef stock.

GAME ONION-HORSERADISH MEATLOAF

2 eggs
¼ cup chili sauce
¼ cup horseradish
¼ cup uncooked old-
fashioned rolled oats
1 T. Worcestershire sauce

1 tsp. black pepper
2 tsp. garlic salt
1 cup diced onion
1½ lbs. ground game
½ lb. ground pork

In a large bowl, beat eggs. Add chili sauce, horseradish, oats, Worcestershire sauce, garlic salt and pepper. Combine well. Add onion and meat and mix well. Place mixture in a loaf pan. Bake at 375° for 45 minutes. Let rest for 5 minutes. Cut and serve.

The reason I add pork is for flavor, as wild game is lean.

WOODSMEN'S PIE

8 medium potatoes
½ cup sour cream
1 tsp. ground nutmeg
1 lb. ground game meat
½ lb. ground pork
1 cup diced onion
2 cloves garlic, minced
1 cup diced red peppers

1 cup diced fresh mushrooms
2 tsp. onion salt
1 tsp. paprika
1 tsp. chili powder
½ tsp. freshly ground black pepper
2 15-oz. cans cream-style corn
1 cup shredded Cheddar cheese

Peel potatoes. Cut into wedges. Cook in salted water until tender. Drain and let moisture steam off. Add sour cream and nutmeg and mash. Set aside, uncovered.

Place ground game, ground pork, onions and garlic in a heavy skillet and brown well. Stir occasionally to keep meat browning evenly. When brown, drain off fatty liquid. Add red peppers, mushrooms, onion salt, paprika, chili powder and black pepper. Combine well. Cover and remove from heat. Let steep for 10 minutes.

In a casserole dish, place meat. Add creamed corn and spread evenly. Top corn with mashed potato mixture. Sprinkle shredded cheddar cheese over potatoes and bake, uncovered, for 30 minutes at 350°, until hot all the way through and potatoes have a light brown crust.

I love mine with dill pickles and garlic toast.

HINTS

You may top meatloaf before baking with ½ cup barbecue sauce.

The reason you drain off liquid from cooked meat is to remove strong game flavor that comes from the fat. You may use any cooked vegetable you wish instead of creamed corn.

WILD GAME PIZZA

1 cup red pepper rings
1 cup green pepper rings
2 cups quartered fresh mushrooms
1½ cups sliced zucchini
1 T. olive or vegetable oil
2 cups ground venison, elk or caribou (red game meat)
dough for 1 pizza crust (see recipe p. 187)
3 cups pizza sauce
2 tomatoes, sliced ½″ thick
2 cups sliced venison sausage links
1 cup sliced olives (black or green)
2 cups shredded mozzarella cheese
1 bulb roasted garlic (see recipe p. 64)

HINT

If you wish, you can place crust under a broiler or on a grill and brown it on both sides before adding the pizza ingredients. Make sure you spray the rack with a nonstick vegetable spray before browning crust.

Cut red and green peppers into ⅓″ rings or slices. Cut mushrooms into quarters. Cut zucchini into ⅓″ rounds. In a large frying pan, heat oil. Add vegetables and sauté until almost tender. Remove from heat to a large bowl to keep. Add ground wild game meat to the hot pan and cook until done. Drain off excess fat.

Lightly grease one large baking sheet. Spread the pizza crust dough into pan. Spread 1 cup pizza sauce on top. Top sauce with vegetables, spreading evenly. Top vegetables with sliced tomatoes. Place cooked wild game meat on top of tomatoes. Pour remaining 2 cups pizza sauce over the top. Top this with venison sausage and olives. Top with mozzarella cheese. Place roasted garlic bulb in center.

Bake pizza at 375° for 30 minutes. Cut into six pieces and serve.

QUICK AND EASY GAME STIR-FRY

1 lb. game meat, cut into 3″ × ½″ × ½″ strips
½ cup chicken stock (see recipe p. 186)
1 T. cornstarch
1 T. vegetable oil
1 cup sliced onion, ¼″ strips
1 cup peeled and sliced celery
1 cup sliced carrots
1 cup snow pea pods, fresh or frozen
½ cup sliced green onions
¼ cup soy sauce
1 T. diced fresh ginger

Remove all bones, fat and silver skin from meat. Cut meat into pieces the size of your little finger.

Cut all vegetables as directed and measure out all liquids. Combine chicken stock with cornstarch.

In a large nonstick skillet, heat oil until almost smoke hot. Add game and brown on all sides. Remove meat, leaving oil. Place meat in covered bowl. Add onions, celery and carrots and sauté until onions and celery are clear. Add pea pods, green onions, soy sauce, ginger and browned meat. Simmer for 2 minutes. Add cornstarch/chicken stock mixture and mix well. Simmer over medium heat until slightly thickened and liquid is clear.

Serve with white rice or wild rice. This also hits the spot over baked potatoes.

HINT

This works well with all game and fowl. I also toss in some shrimp just for fun.

BLACK BEER AND GAME STEW

1½ lbs. red game meat cut into 1" cubes
⅓ cup all-purpose flour
¼ cup olive oil
2 cloves garlic, minced fine
3 cups beef stock (see recipe p. 186)
2 cups dark beer
1 T. molasses
1 tsp. black pepper
2 bay leaves
1 tsp. dry thyme
1 cup cubed carrots, ½" cubes
1 cup cubed turnips ½" cubes
1 cup sliced red potatoes (skins on)
1 cup halved shallots
1 cup green beans, cut in 3" pieces
1 cup quartered mushrooms

Serves 8 hunters

Remove fat and silver skin from meat and cut meat into cubes. Roll cubes in flour. Heat oil in a Dutch oven. Add meat cubes and garlic to the Dutch oven and brown the meat. Add remaining flour and combine with beef stock, beer, molasses, black pepper, bay leaves and thyme.

Cover and bake in a 350° oven for 1 hour. Add carrots, turnips and potatoes and bake ½ hour longer. Gently stir to keep from sticking. Add beans and mushrooms and bake for 20 minutes longer. Remove bay leaves.

Serve with baking powder biscuits.

HINT

Frozen green beans also work well in this recipe.

Game Liver with Bacon Raspberry Vinaigrette
Side dish: Grandma Schumacher's Hashbrowns

Game Liver with Bacon Raspberry Vinaigrette

8 game livers, sliced ½" thick
2 cups milk
6 strips bacon, diced ½"
1 cup sliced onion
1 cup sliced red peppers
¼ cup raspberry vinegar

1 tsp. beef base
¼ cup clarified butter
(see recipe p. 172)
1 cup seasoned flour (add salt
and pepper)

Serves 4

Remove all skin and veins from liver. (This is very important.) Slice and soak livers overnight in milk. In a skillet, cook bacon over medium heat. Add onions and peppers and cook until tender. Combine vinegar and beef base, and add to vegetables. Bring to a boil and reduce heat. Simmer for 3 minutes. Set aside.

Remove liver from milk. Pat dry with paper towels. In a second skillet, heat butter until almost smoke hot. Dredge liver slices in flour. Shake off excess. Add to butter and brown on both sides. Add onion and bacon mixture. Bring to a boil and serve.

If you can't find raspberry vinegar, red wine vinegar works equally well.

HINT

You can use liver from fowl the same way. I keep all my bird livers to use this way.

Wild Mushroom Vegetable Stew

1½ lbs. game meat, cut into 1" cubes
½ cup all-purpose flour
⅓ cup or butter
1 cup diced turnips
1 cup diced carrots
1 cup diced parsnips
1 cup diced onion

1 cup diced celery
4 cups beef stock or game stock
(see recipe p. 186)
¼ cup tomato purée
3 cups halved shiitake mushrooms
2 tsp. dry marjoram
1 tsp. black pepper

Remove all fat and silver skin from game. Cut game into cubes. Toss in flour and shake off excess flour. In a Dutch oven, heat butter to a fast bubble and brown meat. Add vegetables and cook until tender. Add remaining flour and combine gently.

Add game stock and tomato purée. Cover and bake for 1 hour in a 350° oven. Add mushrooms, marjoram and black pepper and bake 1 hour longer or until meat is tender. Serve with dumplings, spaetzle, rice or noodles.

Any fresh or wild mushrooms will work. The more mushrooms the better.

Game Chef
Reference

The best way to skim is to move the ladle lightly in a circular motion around the pot. If you use a clear glass measuring cup in the microwave, it is easy to see where the butter and milk separate.

You should always weigh the flour for this recipe and not measure it.

CLARIFIED BUTTER

1 lb. butter

This is sometimes known as "drawn butter." Place butter in a saucepan at low heat until it is completely melted. Remove all foam which rises to the top of liquid. Take from heat, and let stand until all milk solids have fallen to the bottom of the pot. With a ladle, remove all clear oil and keep.

You may also use margarine, or ½ margarine and ½ butter. One pound of butter or margarine will yield about 12 ounces, or 1½ cups clarified butter.

ROUX

1 lb. butter or margarine
1 lb. all-purpose flour

In a heavy, 2-quart saucepan or baking dish, melt butter. Stir in flour. Bake for 1 hour in a 375° oven, stirring the mixture every 15 minutes. When cooked, the roux should be golden brown and the consistency of sand.

It is always better to use roux at room temperature. The roux keeps well in the refrigerator or freezer.

Sauces and gravies are two of the most important components of great cooking. Roux thickens sauces and gravies. Although roux is only one of many cooking thickeners, after 20 years of professional cooking I concluded that it is the best.

FRESH BREAD CRUMBS

1 lb. fresh sliced bread

Remove crust from bread. Cut slices in half and add one at a time to blender container. Blend on high. After four half slices, empty container. If you have a food processor, place six slices, one at a time, in the processor at high speed.

Making fresh bread crumbs is an important and often overlooked detail of cooking. Fresh bread crumbs are far superior to prepared crumbs, which become overcooked, dry and tasteless.

BROWN SAUCE

3 oz. (6 T.) butter or margarine
1 cup diced onion
½ cup diced celery
½ cup diced carrots
⅔ cup all-purpose flour

6 cups beef stock (see recipe p. 186),
or double strength game stock
(see hint at right)
¼ cup tomato purée
1 bay leaf
1 tsp. salt
½ tsp. black pepper

HINT

To make double-strength stock, reduce 12 cups to 6 cups by rapidly boiling in a large saucepan.
If you don't have homemade stock, you can use canned broth.

In a heavy saucepan, heat butter to a fast bubble. Sauté vegetables until onion is clear. Add flour and cook over low heat for 2 minutes, stirring often with a wooden spoon or rubber spatula.

Heat stock and add to base, stirring slowly and constantly.

Add tomato purée, bay leaf, salt and pepper. Cook for ½ hour. Adjust flavor and consistency to taste. Strain through a fine strainer and serve.

This is the best base for a great brown gravy. If you have any left over, freeze it in small amounts in freezer bags. As you need more gravy, let bags thaw in refrigerator, heat and serve.

SAUCE VELOUTÉ

3 cups chicken stock (see recipe p. 186),
or double-strength upland game bird
stock (see hint for brown sauce at right)
1 cup half-and-half
½ cup dry white wine
5 oz. roux (see recipe p. 172)

In a saucepan, heat stock, half-and-half and wine to a simmer. Whisk in roux slowly to make a smooth sauce. Simmer over low heat for 30 minutes, just below its boiling point. Stir from time to time, making sure bottom of pan is not scorched.

Remove from heat, and put through a strainer for a smooth, lump-free consistency.

This sauce should be used for uplan game bird but not for roast goose or duck.

HINT

Do not use a stainless steel pot. (The sauce will scorch too easily.) To keep mixture from sticking to the sides and bottom of the pan, stir with a rubber spatula.

BASIC WHITE OR CREAM SAUCE

LIGHT VERSION:
1 quart milk or half-and-half
3 ounces roux (see recipe p. 172)

MEDIUM VERSION:
1 quart milk or half-and-half
4 ounces roux (see recipe p. 172)

HEAVY VERSION:
1 quart milk or half-and-half
6 ounces roux (see recipe p. 172)

In a heavy saucepan, heat milk to a slow boil. With a wire whisk, add roux and whisk smooth. (Avoid touching sides or bottom of pan while whisking.)

Reduce heat to a simmer and cook for 5 minutes. Make sure this sauce is smooth. Strain through a fine strainer or put in a blender for 20 seconds.

MUSHROOM SAUCE

1 T. butter
¼ cup, diced shallots
2½ cups sliced, fresh mushrooms
1 cup dry sherry
3 cups brown sauce (see recipe p. 173)

In a sauté pan, melt butter. Add shallots and sauté until clear. Add mushrooms and toss lightly for 20 seconds. Add sherry and simmer for 3 minutes, or until all mushrooms are lightly cooked. Add brown sauce and bring to a boil. Simmer for 10 minutes and serve.

Brown sauce is the same as pan gravy. Any recipe referred to as "hunter's-style" or "jaeger-style" uses this sauce.

John's Very Best Blender Hollandaise

2 whole eggs and 2 egg yolks (or
¾ cup ultra-pasteurized
homogenized eggs)
1½ tsp. chicken base

1 tsp. lemon juice
4 drops hot sauce
2 cups clarified butter
(see recipe p. 172)

Makes about 2 cups

Put eggs, chicken base, lemon juice and hot sauce in a blender. Mix for 5 seconds on low speed. Place a piece of foil over the blender and form a pocket in the foil. Make a small hole (1/16″ diameter) in the bottom of the pocket. This is to make an even, steady stream of butter so that the butter and egg mixture can form an emulsion.

Heat clarified butter to 140°. (This is the hardest part of the recipe. You cannot guess. Use a food thermometer to measure exactly.) Turn blender to medium speed and add butter to base through foil pocket. Sauce should be lemon-colored and thick.

HINT

Use level teaspoons in this recipe. Take care that the small hole in the bottom of foil pocket does not exceed 1/16″.

Béarnaise Sauce

¼ cup, diced shallots
1 T. crushed peppercorns
1 cup tarragon vinegar

Hollandaise sauce recipe, omitting lemon juice and hot sauce
(see recipe above)
1 tsp. fresh tarragon leaves

Place shallots, peppercorns and tarragon vinegar in a small frying pan and simmer over low heat until liquid is almost evaporated. If you don't have tarragon vinegar, substitute white vinegar with 2 tsp. dry tarragon leaves.

Place shallots and peppercorns in a cheese cloth or dish towel, and squeeze out all the liquid. You should have about 1 tablespoon of shallots and peppercorns.

Now prepare hollandaise sauce, substituting the shallots and peppercorns for lemon juice and hot sauce. Add tarragon leaves to prepared sauce and serve.

I love this sauce with all meat and fish.

RED WINE BARBECUE DEMI-GLAZE

4 cups burgundy wine
2 cups plain barbecue sauce
½ tsp. white pepper

Heat wine in a heavy saucepan, reducing to 1 cup. Add barbecue sauce and white pepper. Simmer over low heat for 5 minutes.

IVORY CAPER SAUCE

<table>
<tr><td>1½ T. butter</td><td>1¼ tsp. salt</td></tr>
<tr><td>¼ cup, diced shallots</td><td>1 pinch white pepper</td></tr>
<tr><td>1½ T. all-purpose flour</td><td>⅔ cup heavy cream</td></tr>
<tr><td>¼ cup dry white wine</td><td>1 large bay leaf</td></tr>
<tr><td>1 tsp. lemon juice</td><td>¼ cup capers, drained</td></tr>
</table>

Melt butter in a sauté pan. Add shallots and sauté until clear. Add flour and reduce heat to medium, stirring with a wooden spoon. Cook for 1 minute. Add white wine, lemon juice, salt, pepper and bay leaf. Simmer for 10 minutes on low heat. (Do not boil.) Remove bay leaf and add cream and capers.

Simmer until cream thickens, then serve sauce as soon as possible.

HORSERADISH SAUCE

½ cup Chef John's Horseradish (see recipe p. 65)
1½ cup mayonnaise
3 T. sugar
1 tsp. Worcestershire sauce
3 drops hot sauce

Chop Chef John's Horseradish fine and strain off excess liquid. Place all ingredients in a bowl and combine very well. Keep in a glass container and refrigerate.

HINTS

Be careful not to reduce the liquid in the first stages of preparing this sauce. Serve the sauce as soon as possible after you have finished making it.

You may also add ½ cup pineapple chunks or seeded jalapeño pepper, or both. This sauce is a must with game roasts and grilled steaks.

Chef John's Barbecue Sauce

½ cup butter
3 cloves garlic, minced
1 cup minced onion
½ cup minced green peppers
¼ cup all-purpose flour
2 cups tomato purée
½ cup dill pickle juice
½ cup dry red wine
3 T. red wine vinegar
1 T. lime juice

2 T. lemon juice
½ tsp. liquid smoke
⅓ cup brown sugar
1 tsp. dry mustard
1 tsp. chili powder
1 tsp. salt
½ tsp. paprika
1 tsp. black pepper
⅓ cup diced dill pickles

HINT

Liquid smoke is very important. Adjust the amount of liquid smoke to your own taste. You may double the recipe and keep excess sauce in the refrigerator for up to two weeks. You can add ½ cup bourbon or 1 jalapeño pepper (seeded and diced).

In a sauce pan, melt butter and sauté onions, green peppers and garlic, until onions are clear and soft. Add flour, and cook for 3 minutes, stirring slowly. Add tomato purée, pickle juice, wine, vinegar, lemon juice, lime juice and liquid smoke. Bring to a simmer.

In a bowl, put brown sugar, dry mustard, chili powder, black pepper, salt and paprika.

Mix well. Add to sauce, and simmer slowly for 20 minutes stirring often. Add diced dill pickles and simmer for 10 minutes longer.

Raspberry Balsamic Vinegar Coulis

1 lb. frozen raspberries and liquid
1 cup balsamic vinegar
1 tsp. chicken base
1 tsp. tarragon leaves

¼ cup raspberry jam
1 T. cornstarch
¼ cup cold water

Place raspberries, balsamic vinegar, chicken base, tarragon and jam in a blender cup and purée on medium speed for 2 minutes. Remove and strain through a fine strainer. It is important to remove the seeds.

Place in sauce pot and simmer on medium heat for 15 minutes. Combine cold water and cornstarch to make a smooth liquid. Add slowly to hot base. Simmer on low heat for 5 minutes or until sauce is clear and shiny.

Remove and cool. Keep in covered container. I put sauce in a plastic squirt bottle to paint plates with coulis as I serve the food.

If frozen raspberries come in a 12-oz. bag, it is okay to use instead of a full pound.

This goes on all game. For some extra zip, add 1 tablespoon minced fresh ginger minced after sauce is cooked.

BARBECUE COLA CHILI SAUCE

1 T. olive oil
½ cup diced onion
1 clove minced garlic
1 cup beef stock (see recipe p. 186)
½ cup cola soda
½ cup chili sauce
⅓ cup tomato purée
2 tsp. red pepper flakes
1 tsp. kosher salt
¼ tsp. freshly ground black pepper

In a saucepan heat oil. Add onions and garlic. Sauté until tender. Add remaining ingredients and simmer over low heat for 30 minutes, uncovered.

GAME TARTAR SAUCE

If you prefer, you can substitute green olives stuffed with pimentos for black olives. This sauce goes very well with all upland fowl, water fowl and of course fish.

1 jalapeño pepper, diced
¾ cup, diced dill pickles
¾ cup, diced black olives
⅓ cup, diced onion
2 cups mayonnaise
1 T. sugar

1 T. fresh lemon juice
2 tsp. mustard
1 tsp. dry tarragon leaves
1 tsp. coarsely ground black pepper
1 tsp. Worcestershire sauce
4 drops hot sauce

Remove seeds and stem from jalapeño pepper. Dice crisp dill pickles, black olives and onion, and place in a strainer. Drain well.

In a mixing bowl, combine mayonnaise, sugar, lemon juice, mustard, tarragon leaves, pepper, Worcestershire sauce and hot sauce. Mix well. Add pickles, black olives, onions and jalapeño peppers and gently fold in. (If you prefer, you can substitute green olives stuffed with pimientos for black olives.)

Keep covered sauce in refrigerator. It should keep for one week.

Brown Mustard Brandy Sauce

½ cup brandy
¼ cup brown German mustard
¼ cup packed brown sugar
¼ cup Worcestershire sauce

¼ cup olive oil
2 cloves garlic, mashed
½ tsp. black pepper, freshly ground

Place all ingredients in a blender and purée for 30 seconds. Place meat in a glass bowl and cover with liquid. Cover bowl tightly. I recommend marinating meat in sauce for 24-72 hours in the refrigerator before grilling.

Use leftover marinade to baste the meat while cooking.

Orange Cranberry Sauce

2 cups orange juice
1 lb. fresh cranberries
1 tsp. grated orange zest

1¾ cups sugar
1 T. cornstarch

In a saucepan, place orange juice, cranberries and zest. Bring to a simmer. Mix together sugar and cornstarch, and add to orange-cranberry mixture. Simmer for 5 minutes, until liquid becomes clear and shiny.

Serve warm or chill.

If you wish, you can add 1/4 cup Triple Sec or Cointreau in the first step, for extra flavor.

Pineapple Ginger Chutney

1 T. olive oil
1 cup cubed red onion, ½" cubes
1 clove garlic, minced
1 cup cubed red peppers, ½" cubes
4 cups pineapple chunks
(fresh is best)
½ cup raisins

¼ cup balsamic vinegar
¼ cup packed brown sugar
1 T. cubed fresh ginger, ¼" cubes
1 tsp. black pepper
1 T. chopped fresh mint (optional)
½ cup cold water
2 T. cornstarch

HINT

This goes well with everything. If you like, you may add a diced seeded jalapeño pepper.

In a heavy pot, heat oil. Add red peppers, onions and garlic and sauté until onions are tender, about 5 minutes. Stir to keep from sticking. Add remaining ingredients except for water and cornstarch. Simmer for 15 minutes on low heat, stirring occasionally. Dissolve cornstarch in ½ cup cold water. Add to base. Stir well. Simmer for 10 minutes or until sauce is clear. Remove from heat.

Cool and store in glass container. Keeps up to 1 month in refrigerator.

SAVORY HONEY GLAZE

½ cup dill pickle juice
1 cup brown sugar
1 T. prepared yellow mustard
½ tsp. ground cloves
¼ tsp. ground cinnamon
½ cup maple syrup

1 cup pineapple juice
½ cup chopped onion, cubed
¼ tsp. cayenne pepper
¼ cup cornstarch
½ cup honey

Place all ingredients in a blender and blend until smooth. Place mixture in a heavy saucepan and bring to a slow boil. Simmer for 5 minutes over low heat. Use with game hens, fowl or chops.

MARTINI MARMALADE MARINADE

1½ cups olive oil
1 cup gin
½ cup orange marmalade
¼ cup white vermouth
2 cloves garlic

1 tsp. dry basil
1 tsp. dry tarragon
1 tsp. freshly ground black pepper
1 tsp. salt

Place all ingredients in blender. Blend for 1 minute on low speed. This marinade is to be used with upland game birds. Place game in glass bowl. Cover with marmalade marinade. Let meat marinate for 3 days (no more, no less). Remove meat, leaving marinade on game and grill game over medium heat. Always grill bone side down first.

GREEN PEPPERCORN-CAPER LEMON BUTTER

1 lb. salted butter
1 T. grated lemon juice
2 tsp. lemon zest

1 T. capers, drained
1 T. green peppercorns
3 drops hot sauce

Warm butter to room temperature. Squeeze juice. Place butter, lemon juice and zest in a blender and purée fine.

In a mixing bowl, combine all ingredients. With a large spoon, mix all ingredients well.

Make paper log by placing a sheet of waxed paper one foot long on a flat surface. Place butter on waxed paper 3″ from the bottom. Form into a log. Roll waxed paper into a cylinder. Freeze in a plastic bag and cut off as needed.

HINT

I love this on steak or grilled game bird. Also, this recipe works very well with fish.

CARROT-PEAR COULIS

2 cups cubed carrots, 1″ cubes
1 cup pear liquid
1 T. arrowroot
2 cups pear halves or pieces
2 T. cornstarch

Peel and cube carrots and cook, uncovered, in pear liquid until very tender. When carrots are tender, mix arrowroot with ½ cup pear liquid and return to carrots. Cook over low heat until thick and clear. Place all ingredients in a blender and purée until smooth.

Strain through a fine strainer and keep refrigerated.

ROASTED RED PEPPER COULIS

4 large roasted red peppers (see recipe p. 189)
2 T. olive oil
½ cup chopped shallots
2 cloves garlic, minced
1 T. dill pickle juice
1 T. Worcestershire sauce
¼ cup dry red wine
½ tsp. black pepper
1 tsp. salt

Roast peppers. Remove skin, stem and seeds. Dice into large pieces.
Heat oil hot in a heavy sauté pan. Add shallots and garlic. Sauté over medium heat until shallots are soft and clear. Add peppers. Cover and bake in a 375° oven for 30 minutes. Add remaining ingredients and bring to a boil. Place in a blender and purée until smooth. Strain through a fine strainer. To help sauce through the strainer, tap side of strainer with a wooden spoon. Keep refrigerated.

HINT

If you don't have shallots, onions will be fine. Serve this sauce with upland game birds or grilled steaks.

BLUEBERRY CHUTNEY

*1 orange zest, julienne and juice
1 lemon, juiced
1 cup diced onion
½ cup packed brown sugar
¼ cup red wine vinegar
1 T. molasses
1 qt. fresh blueberries
2 cups strawberries
1 cup golden raisins
½ cup shredded carrots
2 tsp. diced fresh ginger
1 tsp. salt
½ tsp. ground cinnamon
¼ tsp. ground cloves*

Remove zest from orange with a potato peeler. Cut into 1″ matchsticks. Squeeze out the juice for the orange and lemon and remove the seeds.

In a heavy saucepan, bring orange juice, lemon juice, onion, brown sugar, vinegar and molasses to a boil. Simmer over medium heat for 5 minutes, until onions are tender.

Add remaining ingredients and simmer slowly for 15 minutes. Stir from time to time to keep from sticking. Cool.

Keep in a glass container.

JAMAICA JERKED SEASONINGS

*¼ cup allspice berries
1½ cups minced onions
10 green onions, minced
(including tops)
¼ cup dark rum*

*3 hot peppers (Scotch bonnets)
1 cinnamon stick
2 tsp. ground nutmeg
1 tsp. salt
1 tsp. freshly ground black pepper*

Roast allspice berries at 350° for 5 minutes. This brings out the flavor. Place all ingredients in a food processor and make a paste.

For cooking, rub seasoning on meat. Store overnight in a plastic bag.

*Scotch bonnets are
also called Jamar
Hots. They are a
9 on a scale from
1-10. You may
substitute green
jalapeños if
desired. They are
a 5.5 on the scale.*

STRAWBERRY SALSA

2 pts. fresh strawberries
1 cup apple juice
½ cup golden raisins
1 T. red wine vinegar
1 T. lemon juice
2 T. brown sugar
1½ T. cornstarch
½ cup sliced green onions
1 T. diced fresh ginger

Clean and stem berries. Cut in half. In a saucepan, heat apple juice, raisins, red wine vinegar and lemon juice, and bring to a simmer for 5 minutes. Combine brown sugar with cornstarch (no lumps). Add to liquid along with strawberries, green onions and ginger. Simmer until liquid is clear, about 3-4 minutes.

Remove and keep in a covered glass container.

CRANRAISIN RELISH

2 oranges
1 lb. dried cranberries
½ cup orange juice concentrate
1 cup water
2 T. balsamic vinegar
1 cup sugar
2 T. cornstarch

Wash and remove stem from oranges. Cut into ½" slices and remove the seeds. Grind or chop slices until medium fine (no big pieces). Set aside.

Place cranberries, orange juice concentrate, water and vinegar in a pan. Simmer for 20 minutes. Combine the sugar and cornstarch. Add to pan with oranges, stirring well. Simmer for 15 minutes over low heat, stirring often to keep from burning.

HINTS

Cut green onions up about 4" from the bottom. If you can't find fresh ginger, use a hot pepper of your choice.

This can be served hot or cold. It goes with everything. My hardest task is not eating it all as I am cooking it.

MANGO TOMATILLO SALSA

2 qt. fresh tomatillos, diced in ⅓" cubes
1½ cups diced red bell peppers
1½ cups diced red onions
5 mangos, ripe but firm, diced ½"
½ cup chopped cilantro, chopped
½ cup pineapple juice
½ cup lime juice
¼ cup balsamic vinegar
1½ fresh chili peppers, minced
1½ tsp. minced garlic
1½ T. ground cumin

Dice tomatillos, bell peppers, red onions, mangos and cilantro, and place all in a large bowl. Place all remaining ingredients in a blender and purée until smooth. Add to vegetable base. Keep covered and refrigerate up to 1 week.

STRAWBERRY RHUBARB CONFITURE

1 lb. fresh or frozen rhubarb pieces
1 lb. fresh or frozen strawberries
8 oz. frozen lemonade concentrate
1 cup packed brown sugar
2 T. cornstarch

Place rhubarb, strawberries and lemonade in a heavy saucepan and simmer over low heat for 45 minutes. Combine sugar and cornstarch. Add to sauce and simmer for 15 minutes until cornstarch is cooked clear.

Purée sauce in a blender and pour through a strainer to remove rhubarb pulp and strawberry seeds.

To serve, place ½ cup hot sauce on a plate
and top with grilled game or fowl.

HINT

My Father, Big Cull, said "Confiture, my foot! That's strawberry rhubarb sauce." Maybe in 1940, but now it is confiture.

TOMATO SALSA

4 large ripe tomatoes
¼ cup olive oil
¼ cup balsamic vinegar
1 cup diced red onions
2 cloves garlic, minced
½ cup diced green jalapeño
peppers

1 cup diced yellow or red peppers
1 T. brown sugar
1 T. Worcestershire sauce
2 tsp. celery salt
1 tsp. freshly ground pepper
¼ tsp. hot sauce
2 tsp. chopped fresh cilantro

Using fully ripened tomatoes, remove cores and dice into ½″ cubes. In a small saucepan, place olive oil, vinegar, onions and garlic, and cover tightly. Simmer over low heat for about 8-10 minutes. (Do not boil!) Remove from heat and let cool.

Remove seeds and dice jalapeños and yellow peppers.

In a large bowl, combine onion base with brown sugar, Worcestershire sauce, salt, pepper and hot sauce. Add tomatoes, peppers and cilantro and gently mix.

Let stand for at least 2 hours. Serve or refrigerate for later use.

EASY CAESAR DRESSING

¾ cup red wine vinegar
4 oz. anchovy fillets in oil
1 T. yellow mustard
1 T. Worcestershire sauce
1 T. freshly ground black pepper
2 cloves garlic

2 tsp. lemon juice
1 tsp. chicken base
4 drops hot sauce
3 cups olive oil
½ cup shredded Parmesan cheese

HINT

Why 140°? So the oil will pick up the rest of the ingredients for the emulsion.

In a blender, place all ingredients except olive oil and Parmesan cheese. Heat oil to 140°. (This is very important.)

Place a piece of foil on top of the blender and make a deep pocket. Punch a small hole (¹⁄₁₆″ diameter) in the bottom of the pocket. Turn blender on high speed. Pour warm oil into the foil pocket. The dressing will thicken. Remove to a storage container. Add Parmesan cheese and combine well.

Store in covered container in refrigerator.

Brown Game Stock or Beef Stock

5 lbs. game or beef bones
2½ cups onions, coarsely diced
2½ cups diced celery
1½ cups diced carrots

1½ gallons water
2 cups crushed tomatoes
1 sachet bag (see recipe below)

HINT

Do not use leaves or peelings of vegetables in your soup stocks. They will give the stock a bitter taste. If you don't have bones, you can use 5 lbs. bone-in shoulder roast. Beef stock can be made the same way as game stock. By all means, it is okay to use premade or canned stock.

Wash bones and season with salt and pepper. It is best to use bones with some meat on them. Place in a roasting pan. Brown bones in a 375° oven for 1 hour, turning from time to time.

Add onions, celery and carrots and stir. Return to oven and bake until vegetables are golden brown. Place water, bones, drippings and vegetables in a large stock pot. Simmer on low heat for 3 hours. Remove fat and foam as they rise to the surface. Add crushed tomatoes and sachet bag, and simmer for another 3 hours. Skim off fat and foam. Put liquid through a fine strainer. Discard bones and vegetables.

Put liquid back on stove and bring to a fast boil reducing by ⅓.

Chicken Stock

3½ lbs. chicken wings or 1 small
stewing hen
2 cups diced onions
1½ cups diced celery

1½ cups diced carrots
4 quarts water
1 sachet bag

Wash chicken. Place all ingredients in a large soup pot, and simmer on low heat for 3½ hours, skimming off fat and foam from time to time. Remove from heat and strain.

Put only the liquid back in the pot, and return to a fast boil until liquid has been reduced by one-half. Skim off fat, cool and store.

Sachet Bag

1 T. chopped fresh parsley with stems
3 crushed garlic cloves
1 tsp. dry thyme
2 small bay leaves

½ tsp. cracked black peppercorns
4 whole cloves
cheesecloth or tea ball

Makes 1 bag

The purpose of a sachet bag is to produce a balance of seasonings for stocks and soups while being able to remove all spice ingredients when desired.

Place all ingredients in a double-thick cheesecloth or tea ball. Tie cheesecloth loosely with string so the liquid can pass through and extract flavor from its contents.

Pizza Crust

2 cups warm water (a little over 105°)
2 T. dry yeast or two pkgs. yeast
1 tsp. sugar
5 to 6 cups all-purpose flour
2 T. oil
2 tsp. salt

In a large bowl, combine warm water, yeast and sugar. Let stand 2 minutes. Add half the flour, oil and salt. With a large wooden spoon, mix 100 times. Gradually add flour ½ cup at a time, until dough forms a mass and pulls away from the sides of the bowl.

Remove dough to a floured baking cloth. Add ¼ cup flour. If needed, add more flour a little at a time. Knead dough 75 times. Place in greased bowl. Cover with clean cloth.

Set in a warm (not hot) place for one hour. Remove to greased pizza pan. Gently press into desired shape.

Fill crust with desired toppings and bake at 400° until crust is golden brown and crisp.

I like to roll out crust ½ inch thick, spray it with olive oil and grill it on the barbecue. It gives the crust a great flavor.

Butter Pastry Dough for Pot Pies and Meat Pie Covers

¾ cup butter
½ cup cake flour
¼ cup vegetable shortening
1½ cups all-purpose flour
1 tsp. onion salt
½ cup ice-cold water

In a large bowl, combine cake flour, butter and shortening and combine into marble size pieces. Add all-purpose flour and salt and toss into pieces the size of popcorn. Add water and combine to make a stiff dough. Remove from bowl and on a lightly floured cloth knead 30 times. Place in plastic bag and refrigerate for 2 hours to rest. Roll out the size you need.

For a 9 inch pie crust about 8 ounces are needed for the bottom and 7 ounces for the top. For topping only use 8 ounces.

Hints

Try not to make dough too stiff. After you start to knead dough, the more flour you add and the more you knead, the tougher the crust gets.

I use this crust for pot pies or tops of stews. For pot pies, cut rolled dough to the size of the bowl.

Bottom pie crust should weigh 8 ounces. Top crust should weigh 7 ounces for a 9-inch pan.

PIE CRUST

2 cups all-purpose flour
1 tsp. salt
1 1/4 cups vegetable shortening
2/3 cups cold water

In a large bowl, combine flour and salt. (Too much flour will make the crust tough.) Add shortening. Toss to make pieces the size of small marbles. Gradually add ice-cold water, lightly tossing to make a dough. Combine dough just enough to hold together. Use a pastry cloth or dusted board to roll out crust.

For pie shells, poke crust with a fork. Gently shake to shrink dough. Place crust in pie pan; place second pie pan on top. Trim excess dough from edges. Place pans upside down in oven and bake at 350° for 15-18 minutes. This keeps pies from blistering and bubbling. This will make four single-crust or two double-crust 9-inch pies.

Leftover pie crust dough freezes well. Cut into proper weights (see hint) and freeze in individual bags. Always remember to shake crust after putting in a pan. This will help shrink crust before baking.

EGG WASH

2 eggs
1/4 cup milk

Break eggs into a bowl. Add milk. Whisk to a froth. (Never keep egg wash after use as it is a medium for bacteria. If you need a small amount, make half a batch.)

HOW TO CARAMELIZE ONIONS

3 cups sliced onions
1 T. butter
1/4 tsp. salt
1/4 tsp. black pepper
1 1/2 tsp. brown sugar

The key is not to use too much heat. If the heat is too high, onions will burn and become bitter.

Peel and remove the core end of the onions and slice thin. In a heavy skillet, combine all ingredients and cook, uncovered, on low heat for 10 minutes, stirring often. Onions will begin to brown. Continue to cook for another 15-20 minutes, until onions are translucent and golden brown.

Use or cool and keep refrigerated for later use.

TO ROAST PEPPERS

Place peppers on burners and char over flames. When blackened on all sides, transfer to paper bag. Close tightly and let sit to cool for 15 minutes. Remove pepper and brush off skins. If using hot peppers, wear rubber gloves.

BARBECUE GAME RUB

2 tsp. garlic salt
2 tsp. brown sugar
2 tsp. ground cumin
2 T. chili powder
1 T. freshly ground black pepper

½ tsp. cayenne pepper
¼ cup Hungarian paprika
1 tsp. onion powder
olive oil spray

HINT

Rubbed meat should be placed in a bag overnight is to let the dry spices moisten so they don't become a charred black crust.

Mix all ingredients together except olive oil spray making sure there are no lumps. Keep in tightly sealed container. For use, lightly spray meat or fowl with olive oil spray. Rub on spices. Place seasoned meat in a plastic bag and refrigerate overnight. Remove from bag and spray lightly again, then grill. To roast, do the same as for grilling.

NUT CRUST FOR GAME

¾ cup fresh bread crumbs
(see recipe p. 172)
½ cup finely chopped walnuts

¼ cup finely chopped cashews
¼ cup Parmesan cheese
½ tsp. freshly ground black pepper

Combine all ingredients and use as in standard breading procedure.

POPPYSEED DRESSING

1 cup sugar
1 teaspoon salt
½ tsp. white pepper
2 tsp. dry mustard
½ cups white vinegar

2 cups vegetable salad oil
¼ cup onion
2 T. fresh lemon juice
¼ teaspoon black pepper
3 T. poppy seeds

Place all ingredients, except poppy seeds, in a blender container. Blend one minute. Remove from blender, add poppy seeds, and mix well.

This dressing keeps refrigerated up to two weeks. Always shake well before using.

INDEX